DATE DUE		
MAR 2 0 1990		
MAR 2 0 1990		

Ann Beattie

Twayne's United States Authors Series

Warren French, Editor

Indiana University

TUSAS 510

ANN BEATTIE
(1947–   )
Photograph © Thomas Victor, 1985

Ann Beattie

By Christina Murphy

Texas Christian University

Twayne Publishers
A Division of G. K. Hall & Co. • Boston

Ann Beattie

Christina Murphy

Copyright © 1986 by G. K. Hall & Co.
All Rights Reserved
Published by Twayne Publishers
A Division of G. K. Hall & Co.
70 Lincoln Street
Boston, Massachusetts 02111

Copyediting supervised by Lewis DeSimone
Book production by Marne B. Sultz
Book design by Barbara Anderson

First Printing

Typeset in 11 pt. Garamond
by Compset, Inc., Beverly, Massachusetts

Printed on permanent/durable acid-free paper
and bound in the United States of America

Library of Congress Cataloging in Publication Data

Murphy, Christina, 1947–
   Ann Beattie.

   (Twayne's United States authors series ; TUSAS 510)
   Bibliography: p. 132
   Includes index.
   1. Beattie, Ann—Criticism and interpretation.
I. Title.   II. Series.
PS3552.E177Z78   1986   813'.54   86-10303
ISBN 0-8057-7474-2

For Pamela Evans and Amy Whitten, who believed, and without whom life would lose much of its sweetness.

Contents

About the Author

Christina Murphy was born in Newton, Massachusetts, and grew up in Fort Lauderdale, Florida. She received her B. A. from Temple University in Philadelphia, Pennsylvania, and her M. A. and Ph.D. from the University of Connecticut. She has published articles on a variety of figures in American literature including Edgar Allan Poe, Henry Timrod, Walker Percy, Eudora Welty, and Hortense Calisher as well as studies of the theory of rhetoric and composition. She has taught at the University of Mississippi and the University of Southern Mississippi and at present teaches in the English department at Texas Christian University in Fort Worth, Texas.

Preface

Since 1976, Ann Beattie has published three collections of short stories and three novels and has earned a reputation as one of the most distinguished of contemporary writers. Yet, to date, no comprehensive study has appeared to analyze the creative vision underlying Beattie's fictive universe or to consider Beattie's relevance to the contemporary literary period.

This volume seeks to provide a framework for interpreting the themes and philosophical perspectives of Beattie's fiction; to consider the development of Beattie's literary achievement; and to place Beattie within the contexts of the postmodernist and neorealist movements in contemporary fiction. It is predicated on the assumption that Beattie, as the inheritor of the tradition of social realism that extends from Ernest Hemingway to John Cheever and John Updike,[1] is an important figure in the neorealist movement of contemporary literature and, as an accomplished and highly praised writer in her own right, is worthy of extended critical analysis and explication.

Christina Murphy

Texas Christian University

Acknowledgments

I wish to thank the English department of Texas Christian University for providing an atmosphere conducive to scholarship and a camaraderie supportive of personal achievement. Many friends in the department have sustained me throughout the course of this study, most especially Dr. Harry Opperman, whose kindness and encouragement were deeply valued and appreciated.

Ann Beattie kindly shared both correspondence and conversation that assisted me greatly in completing the biographical section of this study, and I wish to thank Ms. Beattie for her help.

Grateful appreciation is expressed to the following for permission to quote from previously published materials: "Dwarf House" and "Snakes' Shoes" by Ann Beattie. Copyright 1975 *The New Yorker Magazine,* Inc. from *Distortions;* reprinted by permission of Doubleday & Company, Inc. "Fancy Flights" by Ann Beattie from *Distortions.* Copyright 1974, 1975, 1976 by Ann Beattie; reprinted by permission of Doubleday & Company, Inc. *Chilly Scenes of Winter* by Ann Beattie. Copyright 1976 by Ann Beattie; reprinted by permission of Doubleday & Company, Inc. *Secrets and Surprises* by Ann Beattie. Copyright 1976, 1977, 1978 by Ann Beattie; reprinted by permission of Random House, Inc. *Falling in Place* by Ann Beattie. Copyright 1980 by Ann Beattie; reprinted by permission of Random House, Inc. *The Burning House* by Ann Beattie. Copyright 1979, 1980, 1981, 1982 by Irony & Pity, Inc.; reprinted by permission of Random House, Inc. *Love Always* by Ann Beattie. Copyright 1985 by Irony & Pity, Inc.; reprinted by permission of Random House, Inc.

Chronology

1982   *The Burning House;* a recut version of *Head over Heels* is released by United Artists as *Chilly Scenes of Winter;* author's telescript of short story "Weekend" prepared for PBS is broadcast on WNET, New York, 20 April; divorced from David Gates in May.

1983   Receives honorary Doctor of Humane Letters degree from American University.

1985   *Love Always.*

Chapter One

From *Distortions* to *Love Always:* A Biography

Prologue

The story begins with a story.

Ann Beattie says she became a writer, in part, because a personnel agency told her she wouldn't get a job without cutting her nails, and she had no intention of doing anything so arbitrary and impersonal.[1] Instead, she entered a Ph.D. program and more or less happened into writing fiction because of the frustration she felt about the way literature was taught in graduate courses.[2] "I never had a burning ambition to become a writer," Beattie has stated. "I started writing because I was bored with graduate school—in some kind of attempt to care about literature again."[3] "I was in graduate school, and I was miserable. So I pushed my desk against the wall and started writing instead of reading criticism about writing all day."[4] She adds that "writing was just sort of a process of elimination. I don't have tremendous skills in a tremendous number of areas. I never really set out to be a writer. I just sort of backed into it. Years ago when I might have done something else, I just didn't pursue it, and now I don't know what else to call myself except a writer."[5]

The story, even if hyperbolic, certainly lends credence to Beattie's contention that, for her, writing is less of a romantic calling than a carefully defined craft. This perception is consistent with critics' varied responses to Beattie's work. Though a great many praise Beattie's style for its stark, precise attention to detail and its lack of emotive resonance, a significant number of critics also envision her writing as nothing more than craft—slickly patterned narratives reflecting the entropy of contemporary art and society. While particular reservations about Beattie's style, themes, or axiological focus have been voiced, few critics deny Beattie's artistic achievement or refute J. D. O'Hara's assessment that Beattie is the most significant author to emerge in contemporary American fiction since Donald Barthelme.[6]

Early Life

Ann Beattie was born in Washington, D.C., on 8 September 1947, the only child of James A. and Charlotte (Crosby) Beattie. Her father was a government official, who became a grants management specialist within the Department of Health, Education, and Welfare, and Beattie has often described her childhood, despite the glamour and diversity of Washington, as a very ordinary one—normal and middle class. "I grew up in the suburbs of Washington, D.C.," she says, "and I was an artsy little thing . . . you know, painting, pictures, writing. I had a good imagination."[7] She attended Lafayette Elementary School and graduated from Woodrow Wilson High School in 1965. She was "something less than an academic whiz-kid in high school," a fact that she attributes to "a combination of boredom, mediocre academic programs and teachers, a lack of interest and understanding." Although she claims that she "wasn't interested in anything in high school,"[8] she did sufficiently well to be admitted to American University. "It wasn't until I got to college," she states, "that I began to take writing seriously—not my own, but literature. I took a course with Frank Turaj, and he taught me how to read. That was the beginning."[9] Early favorites whom she admired and whom critics often find echoes of in her work included F. Scott Fitzgerald, Ernest Hemingway, and John Updike.[10] She graduated from American University with a B.A. in English in 1969.

Graduate School and Marriage

After American University, Beattie entered the graduate program in English at the University of Connecticut, where she went around "pretending to be an expert on Ezra Pound"[11] but was secretly engaged in writing stories. She claims that she started writing seriously—"more than a couple of stories a year"—in 1971.[12] "In those days," she says, "I would write the most fanciful thing I could, like imagining an obese woman who was marrying for the fourth time . . . or spacemen who come to earth to take pornographic pictures. It was fun." She published her first short story, "A Rose for Judy Garland's Casket," in *Western Humanities Review* in 1972. By this time, Beattie had received her M.A. in English from the University of Connecticut and had enrolled in the Ph.D. program. She withdrew from the program in 1972, two preliminary examinations and one dissertation short of achieving her doctorate. "I was saved by the *New Yorker*," she says. "They started to publish me in my mid-twenties, after having rejected twenty stories in a row."[13] "I came in over the transom. No agent or friend, except my manila envelope. It's unusual, I know."[14]

In 1973, Beattie married David Gates, a fellow student she had met at the University of Connecticut. The two were married on 5 June in Eastford, Connecticut, after having lived together on a combined income of six thousand dollars before Beattie proposed. "We played a game in those days," Gates says. "We have written agreements to do things, and she sneaked it into one of the documents."[15] Beattie has acknowledged her husband's contributions to her success, listing him with Roger Angell, her editor at the *New Yorker*, and J. D. O'Hara, a close friend and critic of contemporary fiction, as the three people she most trusts to assess her work and to whom she calls out for help and advice. She also has attributed to her ex-husband a capacity to help her assess accurately the merit of her writing, citing, as an example, her lack of faith in "Snakes' Shoes," a story often cited by critics as one of her finest. "I didn't think 'Snakes' Shoes' amounted to much," Beattie says, "so I tossed it in the pantry, where the garbage piled up. Later my husband asked what happened to the story about the two people who sit on a rock at Hall's Pond. He dug it out, patched it together, and got it off to the *New Yorker*, where it eventually appeared. Sometimes I don't have a clear perspective on my work."[16] The two were divorced in May, 1982.

The Literary Career

In 1976, *Distortions,* a collection of Beattie's early stories that had appeared in the *New Yorker*, the *Atlantic Monthly*, the *Virginia Quarterly Review, Transatlantic Review*, and the *Texas Quarterly*, was published by Doubleday. In that same year, Doubleday also released Beattie's first novel, *Chilly Scenes of Winter*. Both works established for her a prominent position in contemporary letters. The response to Beattie's writings was immediate and intense. Critics lauded *Distortions* for its sparse style and envisioned it as the perfect artistic representation of the values and anxieties of the generation of the sixties—the "Woodstock generation" with its lost idealism and emotional apathy. Jay Parini states that "reviewers were fascinated, but disturbed, by what they read, finding no obvious moral center in Beattie's vision." But Beattie responded that it was not her responsibility to offer a moral nor to give answers to questions she might raise. "Why should I be passing moral judgments?" she asked. "Because there is so little in the way of moral judgment in my work, reviewers feel that I'm detached. They associate this detachment with technology—the ways you can't talk back to a television. They miss the humor in my stories."[17]

Chilly Scenes of Winter, in addition to being a critically well received novel, was also a highly successful work commercially. In 1979, a film version of *Chilly Scenes of Winter,* directed by Joan Micklin Silver, was released by United Artists as *Head over Heels.* Beattie played a small cameo role in the film as a waitress. The film was only moderately successful at the box office and received mixed reviews. John Skow, in *Time* magazine, said, "Let's give three cheers and a quark for *Head over Heels,* an eccentric little comedy about what zoologists call pairbonding,"[18] while Renata Adler, in the *New Yorker,* stated that *Head over Heels* "wastes its first half hour" and then "lives up for a while to its aspirations, before disintegrating toward its close.[19] The film opened in New York in the fall and was withdrawn after five weeks. Beattie has said that the film's title *Head over Heels* "sounded as if Fred Astaire should be dancing across the credits,"[20] and David M. Taylor states that "the movie's conclusion even exceeds Hollywood's usual penchant for happy endings."[21] The film was rereleased in 1982 as *Chilly Scenes of Winter* with an edited ending; the second version was a much more successful product, both artistically and commercially. It became a type of minor cult film in the New England area.

Beattie made several forays into academia while her career as a writer was burgeoning. From 1975 to '77, she served as visiting writer and lecturer at the University of Virginia in Charlottesville, teaching courses in literature and creative writing. During 1977–78, she was the Briggs-Copeland Lecturer in English at Harvard University and taught courses in fiction writing.

Beattie claims that she does not "really care for" teaching fiction writing. "It's not that I dislike teaching. I don't," she says.

What it is, is I get into it too much. When I teach a course in literature, such as I did in Virginia, I somehow can make the separation between literature as I teach it and as I write it. But inevitably, because I'm a classroom personality identified as a writer, it becomes more difficult when I "teach" writing. I just find it hard to write when I see so much writing. When I see it in a book, that doesn't seem to affect me. But when I see 20 bad student stories a week, I think, "Oh there's too much bad writing in the world already." And then I don't do my work either.[22]

Beattie also found the impersonal environment of academia distressing. Of her year teaching at Harvard, she said: "I left without ever meeting the head of the English department. . . . I did not feel important at Harvard."[23]

A Guggenheim Fellowship, awarded in 1978, freed Beattie to work upon her writing. A second volume of short stories, *Secrets and Surprises,* was published in 1979, and a second novel, *Falling in Place,* in 1980. Both works brought Beattie continued critical recognition and a wide popular audience. Mary Vespa states that the publication of *Falling in Place* made Beattie "a major literary figure at the age of 32."[24] In 1980, in recognition of her contributions to contemporary literature, Beattie received an award from the American Academy and Institute of Arts and Letters, and the Distinguished Alumnae Award from her alma mater American University. American University also presented Beattie with an honorary Doctor of Humane Letters degree in 1983.

Beattie published her third collection of short stories, *The Burning House,* in 1982, and her third novel, *Love Always,* in 1985. The achievements of both works further enhanced Beattie's reputation and drew praise for her insight into the contemporary experience.

Of her writing habits, Beattie has commented that she is both eccentric and erratic. She says that she does not adhere to any strict writing schedule and has gone up to six months at a time without writing anything. "I doubt any schedule would help me," she says. "I do think of writing as being mysterious, so I can't conceive of being mysterious from, say, 9:00 a.m. to noon. When I do write, it's almost always late at night. That's not as odd as it seems. I just don't key-up until late in the day. That's when I'm most energetic."[25] She adds that "I've always had what people call 'writers' block,' but it's never scared me because I never thought of it as that. My total output is pretty large and I can't be too frightened about deviating from work habits that have always never been a routine." Of the "mundane details" of her writing, she says,

I always work at a typewriter. I can make some revisions or do fine editing in longhand, but if I'm revising a whole page I always go back to the typewriter. . . . I'm also very neurotic about my work habits. To this day I have my mother mail to me, from Washington D.C., a special kind of typing paper—which isn't even particularly *good* typing paper—from People's Drug Store. It costs about $1.29 a pack. I used to always work in my husband's clothes. He's not my husband any longer, but I still occasionally put on the essential plaid shirt.[26]

When the *New York Times Book Review* asked Beattie to name the writers who had most affected her work, Beattie responded,

This is a hard question to answer, at the risk of flattering myself. I don't think I write like any other writer. I started writing seriously when I was in graduate school studying literature. In those days, the only modern writer I recall thinking a lot about was Samuel Beckett. I'd always been attached to certain works by F. Scott Fitzgerald and Ernest Hemingway. In the late 1960's, I started reading contemporary fiction. I much admired John Updike. (While I'm flattered by comparisons critics now make between our work, he's accomplished much more than I could manage; I could never be so careful and yet keep my stories so uncontrived.) Other writers who knocked me over (whom I met in *Esquire*) were Joy Williams and Raymond Carver. I suppose I learned from them that it was O.K. to write about extraordinary things buried within the mundane, to let my sense of humor show, and that if you surprised the characters, you'd surprise the reader."[27]

In an interview in the *Literary Review,* Beattie added that other contemporary writers she enjoys and admires are Mary Lee Settle, Donald Barthelme, whom she considers "the true genius of our time," Anne Tyler, Tobias Wolff, Stanley Crawford, and Steven Millhauser. "If there's one story I could die happy having written," she states, "it's 'What Is It?' by Raymond Carver. If there's one novel I could have written, it would have been Steven Millhauser's *Edwin Mullhouse.*"[28]

"I basically write because I think it's fun," Beattie comments, observing, "my stories always seem to begin with something very small."

If I were to say I usually begin with a character, that wouldn't mean that I would know the character's occupation or whether the character is happy or sad, or what the character's age was. I *would* know that the character is named "Joe," and, yes, sometimes the idea that the character's name is "Joe" has gotten me to the typewriter. More often it's really a physiological feeling that I should write something. . . . Something in me has built up and this is a compulsion to go and write something at the typewriter. And, yes, it's not totally amorphous, there is something in the back of my mind: it's a name, it's a sentence, it's a sense of remembering what it is like to be in the dead of winter and wanting to go to the beach in the summer, some vague notion like that. It's never more than that. I've never in my life sat down and said to myself, "Now I will write something about somebody to whom such-and-such will happen."[29]

Beattie also maintains that the writing process is a mysterious one for her and not one she is eager to unravel or understand. "I've been absolutely shocked in classrooms where I've heard my stories discussed," she says. "Sometimes I've been so enlightened, I've taken notes. But now I've gotten to the point where indeed I'm informed, but want to forget about that enlightenment immediately. A while ago, for example, my editor at the *New Yorker* wrote to say he thought a story I'd written was good, but he wanted some changes. He mentioned that I often used scenes in restaurants to mark time . . . and I was horrified to be told that. I just don't want to get hung up by knowing too much about what I'm doing."[30]

In assessing the contemporary literary period, Beattie sees contemporary fiction as being profoundly influenced by film. "In my cynicism," Beattie states,

I usually say film is way ahead of literature. Right now, this may not be so true. A decade ago, film was clearly leading. But there's a new undercurrent. . . . I think you can be more subtle about allusions in writing than you can when presenting them visually in a film. You can hide them in a book or story easier. Writers seem to better understand the necessity of transforming something from the visual to the written. . . . I think, too, the fictional forms are gaining in depth and variety in terms of film. The classic case was nineteenth century painting versus the advent of photography. People didn't just pack up their paints. Painting moved in entirely new directions. I see a latter day parallel in the relationship between fiction and film. Perhaps another way to say it is that today's fiction is more refractive, less reflective.

Her overall assessment of her own writing and of the writing of the contemporary period is that "fiction is becoming increasingly dark, deeper, subtle and more mysterious than ever before."[31]

Chapter Two
The Literary Milieu
The Postmodernist Influence

Although Ann Beattie's fiction emerged during the postmodernist period, technically Beattie is not a postmodernist writer. According to Mas'ud Zavarzadeh, postmodernism represented "a new distribution of narrative energy in post–World War II American literature."[1] It developed as a reaction to the totalizing impact of modernist fiction—in which the writer "interpreted the 'human condition' in the light of a comprehensive private world view."[2] While modernism (generally regarded as the major literary movement between 1900 and 1945 and represented by such authors as James Joyce, William Faulkner, D. H. Lawrence, and Virginia Woolf) placed a high emphasis upon interiority, or the capacity of the individual consciousness—usually that of the artist or the poet—to make meaning from a fragmented and enervated exterior social reality, postmodernism revealed a general "mistrust of the epistemological authority of the interpretive novel" largely because the complexities of contemporary society made "all interpretations of 'reality' arbitrary and therefore at the same time both accurate and absurd."[3] As Zavarzadeh states in *Mythopoeic Reality*, "In this post-absurd world, daily experience eludes simple meaningful/meaningless reality testing; it is, in Robbe-Grillet's words, 'neither significant nor absurd. It *is*, quite simply.'"[4] Thus, the postmodernists developed a flat, expressionless narrative style to encompass reality as "it *is*, quite simply" rather than to interpret reality by means of a strong narrative voice and a defined philosophical attitude (as seen in modernist fiction). Thus, too the emphasis upon value-free or value-neutral fiction in postmodernism, a focus that has caused many critics to view the movement as a perfect literary reflection of the realities of a "technetronic society—a society that is shaped culturally, psychologically, socially, and economically by the impact of technology and electronics—particularly in the area of computers and communications."[5] As Zavarzadeh suggests:

The new communication technologies make the formulation of any encompassing authoritative visions increasingly more difficult, since they produce an information overload which gives such diverse and disparate views of reality that no single interpretive frame can contain them all and still present a coherent vision of experience. The information revolution also expands the range of the probable to the extent that it blurs the boundaries of fact and fiction with the ultimate effect, as far as the conventional novel is concerned, being that the contemporary reader feels uneasy entering the world of the totalizing novel rooted in the dualistic epistemology of the actual and the imaginal. Unlike the novel of the industrial age, the postbourgeois novel favors the technique of "collage" for the organization of experience rather than "plot." Collage, typographical enactments, and innovative uses of paginal space are more in accord with contemporary man's exposure to the multilayered nature of experience in the new age and the ambivalent attitude that experience engenders in defiance of being compressed into an epiphanic whole.[6]

Annie Dillard in *Living by Fiction* describes this type of writing as "art without a center," in which "the world is an undirected energy; it is an infinite series of random possibilities" in which "the world's coherence derives not from a universal order but from any individual stance."[7] It is appropriate to see postmodernism, therefore, as not only an innovation in the history of narrative but as a rebellion against modernism in particular and mimetic art in general. Postmodernism is an important literary movement not only for its profound effect upon the shape of contemporary writing, but for the fact that it attempted to redefine the mimetic tradition and to establish that nonmimetic literature has a valid aesthetic. As such, it represents an epistemological break with the past and indicates a new literary mythography.

Mimesis and Antimimesis

Traditional mimetic fiction depends upon an implicit contract between the writer and the reader that the world the writer creates in fiction is recognizable to the reader and that its motives, values, perspectives, and actions are intelligible or interpretable to the reader. Readers perceive a world in the fiction that they assume corresponds to the world that they live in, which is their reality. Reality in mimetic fiction is regarded as set and external, based largely upon the eighteenth-century model of fixed universal laws and a linear sense of the universe as progressing steadily through space and time. Because reality is set and external, it is also ultimately knowable; thus, philosophical perspectives, moral stances, and axiological foundations are not only possible within mimesis but generally are the standard fare of mimetic fiction.[8]

Mimetic fiction began to be defined as a tradition in the early eighteenth century, and it was not until the mid-twentieth century that the comfortable assumptions of mimetic fiction were profoundly challenged by postmodernism. Postmodernism offered not only nonmimetic fiction to its readership but a new paradigm for understanding the fiction-making process. "Literature," Roland Barthes comments, "is neither an instrument nor a vehicle; it is a structure,"[9] and postmodernist writers set out to explore the structures of fiction independent of their relevance or relationship to the structures and assumptions of external reality. The assertion in postmodernism was that literature is its own reality, that fictional systems are indeed *fictional,* and that, therefore, they should operate in accord with their own aesthetic values and internal ordering patterns. As symbol systems, fictions need not address any reality other than their own internal consistency—they need not, in essence, correspond to the world of external reality nor comment upon that world if they do not see the necessity or relevance of such a perspective.

Metafiction/Surfiction: The Design of Postmodernism

At the time Ann Beattie was formulating the tenets of her fiction, postmodernism had established both an ethos and an aesthetic for nonmimetic literature. The philosophy, known variously as metafiction or surfiction, advocated the primacy of the artistic imagination and the right of the artist to generate expressive, creative visions unbounded by socio-realistic concerns. Metafictionists, like Donald Barthelme, John Barth, William Gass, and Robert Coover, were essentially experimentalists challenging the conventional assumptions of representational art and endeavoring to have fiction considered on its own terms as an aesthetic artifice rather than as a mimetic reflection of external reality.

"A weariness with worn-out fictional conventions was partly responsible," Joe David Bellamy contends; "the new writing indicated that fiction was at last catching up with the waves of innovation and consolidation that had already taken place decades before in other less refractory arts such as painting, music, or film."[10] Bellamy argues that "just as photography helped turn painters away from representation-alism . . . so film, TV, and the new journalism conspired to deflect serious fiction writers away from realism. When it comes to represent-ing *things,* the argument goes, one picture *is* worth a thousand words, and one movie may be worth a trillion. Having lost out in the contest to 'represent reality,' fiction could survive only if it abandoned 'reality' altogether and turned instead to the power of words to stimulate the imagination."[11]

Once metafictionists had shifted the locus of fiction from the exter-nal world to the imagined world—the mind of the artist as the su-prastructure, the repository of all rules, principles, and frameworks—the issue for postmodernism essentially became how far literature, as a context-dependent pattern, could go into the realm of individuation and still retain intelligibility. Ronald Sukenick describes the surfic-tional phenomenon of attempting to make the constitutive principles of the imagination equivalent to the ordering principles of reality in this fashion: "The mind orders reality not by imposing ideas on it but by discovering significant relationships within it, as the artist abstracts and composes the elements of reality in significant integrations that are works of art."[12] The desire of the surfictionists was to make litera-ture a pure art form, equal to art and music, in being free from socie-tally-determined contexts of meaning and responsive only to the creative powers of the artist in determining both meaning and form.

Surfiction and the Limits of Nonrepresentational Fiction

The attempt in surfiction to distance language from its referent (reality)—in essence to generate a nonreferential type of literature as pure message without the restrictions of context—represents the limits of intelligibility within fictive expression. Once these limits had been tested and art had been generated by removing referential restraints, there was, quite truly, no place further for postmodernist literature to go as a radical movement reacting to the constraints of the mimetic tradition.

Once surfiction and postmodernism had established the design of the antimimetic rebellion, it was perhaps inevitable that postmodern-ism itself would generate the seeds of its own reactionary movement by establishing, in Hegelian fashion, the antithesis to its own concepts and concerns. In physics, the law of an equal reaction for every action is a constant, and such consistency of response seems to hold true for literary movements as well. One could almost assume that if postmodernism developed as a reaction to the mimetic tradition, the reaction to postmodernism itself would be a revolt against antimimesis, establishing a type of alternative mimetic literature that would displace postmodernism as the predominant literary mode. In contemporary literature, roughly the period of 1970 to the present, such a rebellion did occur, but the return to the mimetic tradition was heavily marked by postmodernist influences. The literary movement that followed postmodernism is generally designated as minimalism, and it is to this movement, not to postmodernism, that Ann Beattie as a writer belongs.

Minimalism, or the Response to Postmodernism

If the movement that followed postmodernism were placed in the context of the historical linearity generally favored by critics, that movement would be known as "post-postmodernism" or "pre-neo-realism"; as it is, the movement is known by the unfortunate designation of "minimalism," a term that has pejorative connotations.

Minimalism originated as a concept to designate a movement in the contemporary plastic arts that emphasized the use of small spaces as integers within the thematics of painting and sculpture.[13] The focus of minimalism was upon the use of space itself as a counterpoint to line, or artistic intent. Space was perceived as a "free" medium (one not affected by intent) and the desired effect in minimalist art was to combine intentional design with nonintentional space so that the nonintentional or "free" medium could give greater shape, and thus more import, to the intentional aspects of a work.

In literature, the equivalent emphasis would be upon silence (or what is not said or narrated in a fiction) as the "free" medium, and narration (or what is said) as the intentional sphere. By using what is not said in a narrative as the counterpoint to what is said, what *is* narrated in a story (essentially the art of the story itself) is made more pronounced, more direct, and more intense.

In minimalist fiction, as practiced by Ann Beattie, Raymond Carver, and Frederick Barthelme, among others, there is a persistent focus upon cutting away from fiction all that need not be there to "tell" the story. Critics of minimalist fiction call this emphasis a reduction in scope, while advocates envision this directed energy as a refinement of the art work itself, making contemporary literature more focused, more precise, more perceptive of the telling details that speak volumes. From this perspective, minimalist fiction becomes a type of narrative scrimshaw or a form of literary pointillism emphasizing the precision of fine details used accurately and skillfully for meaningful, emotive impressions.

If postmodernism can be viewed as reducing the influence of subjectivity upon the shape and texture of fictional forms, it is apparent that minimalism, as an outgrowth of postmodernism, would retain the bias against in-depth psychological probings of characters and situations that the postmodernists hold. It is apparent, too, that critics who favor the mimetic tradition—with its strong emphasis upon psychological portrayals as the thematic center from which meaning emerges—would look with disfavor upon the reduction of fiction's range of vision from the deep structures of the mind in conflict with reality to an emphasis upon (as these critics see it) only surface assessments of reality.

Joshua Gilder, in a strident attack upon minimalist fiction, claims that minimalist authors "seem intent on proving the proposition that less is, indeed, less." "Anyone who reads the *New Yorker*," Gilder contends, "will be familiar with minimalist fiction: those little stories which seem to grow even smaller as you read."[14] Citing Ann Beattie, Raymond Carver, Mary Robison, Tobias Wolff, John L'Heureux, and Alice Munro as examples of minimalist writers, Gilder claims that the emphasis in minimalism upon "miniaturized epiphanies" implies that "things like plot and character development have no place here; they imply movement, and the only movement allowed in these stories is a steady constriction of vision, a tighter and tighter hold on reality until finally all life is squeezed out and the pulse stops."[15]

Gilder's analysis of minimalism consists of criticizing minimalist writers for detailing the lives of characters unable to make moral choices while praising contemporary writers like James Ferry, Charles Baxter, and William Hauptman for producing stories that are "religious" in the sense that "they try to find some meaningful order in experience."[16] Distilled, Gilder's argument favors a literature that presents a moral perspective upon life—one that offers solutions to ethical dilemmas and difficult emotional choices rather than one that simply presents images of life elaborated from a philosophically neutral stance.

The counter to Gilder's assumption that literature must comment upon life and offer viable moral options is the aesthetic perspective, held by both postmodernist and minimalist authors, that literature, as an artifice, need only be consistent and faithful to its own imaginative vision.

In the contemporary period, the author and critic who has most championed the cause of moral criticism is John Gardner, who states in *On Moral Fiction:*

Nothing could be more obvious, it seems to me, than that art should be moral and that the first business of criticism, at least some of the time, should be to judge works of literature (or painting or even music) on grounds of the production's moral worth. . . . True art is by its nature moral. We recognize true art by its careful, thoroughly honest search for and analysis of values. It is not didactic because, instead of teaching by authority and force, it explores, open-mindedly, to learn what it should teach. It clarifies, like an experiment in a chemistry lab, and confirms. As a chemist's experiment tests the laws of nature and dramatically reveals the truth or falsity of scientific hypotheses, moral art tests values and rouses trustworthy feelings about the better and the worse in human action.[17]

One of Gardner's central concerns in *On Moral Fiction* is to take postmodernist and minimalist writers to task for trivializing art by providing images of the contemporary scene but no ethical or philosophical framework with which to assess those images. Gardner's view is that postmodernist and minimalist writers do not produce what he considers "true" art or moral art, and his position is essentially this: "I do not deny that art, like criticism, may legitimately celebrate the trifling. . . . But trivial art has no meaning or value except in the shadow of more serious art, the kind of art that beats back monsters and, if you will, makes the world safe for triviality. That art which tends toward destruction, the art of nihilists, cynics, merdistes, is not properly art at all. Art is essentially serious and beneficial, a game played against chaos and death, against entropy."[18]

Gardner's attack upon the limitations of postmodernist and minimalist art is an extensive and forceful expression of a sentiment that pervades the criticism of minimalist fiction and that has a profound effect upon assessments of Ann Beattie and Raymond Carver as the foremost writers of the movement. Traditionally, mimetic fiction has concerned itself with the full panoply of the human drama, focusing upon humanity's interior psychological struggles as well as its struggles with society and nature. In the midst of depicting these immense struggles, mimetic authors were expected to present moral solutions and to uphold moral and spiritual values. Considering the artistry and concerns of minimalism, it is apparent that its writers are operating within the mimetic tradition but not within its traditional boundaries and definitions.

The concern in minimalism is not with the panoply but with the particular—with what Joan Didion has described as the "window on the world"[19]— and many critics, often with much hostility, regard such a defection from conventional mimetic stances and concerns as a betrayal of a noble tradition; thus, many are reluctant, like Gardner, to regard minimalism as a literary movement of much substance or worth.

Ann Beattie herself has commented that "I certainly don't feel it's the obligation of *any artist* to supply answers."[20] Jay Parini's assessment of minimalism and of Beattie's fiction is that "writers are not social historians and their responsibility has much more to do with catching universal meanings in a particular place or person than in surveying a broad scene,"[21] and David M. Taylor remarks of Beattie's fiction that "it is not unexpected that a writer who says her stories offer no answers because she doesn't believe there are any answers to offer would shy from neatly resolved conflicts."[22]

Yet it is often the absence of "neatly resolved conflicts" that critics like Joshua Gilder deplore so strongly in Beattie's fiction, indicating once more that criticisms of Beattie's work are often directed less at the quality of her work per se than at her work's lack of congruence with the conventions and values of the mimetic tradition. For the classic metaphor of mimetic literature as a mirror reflecting social realities, minimalist writers, especially Beattie, would propose the metaphor of literature as a Mobius strip, a literature that captures and reflects reality along one plane and then folds that reflection in upon itself for another entirely new perspective upon reality and art; a literature that sees the reflecting of social realities not as a simple, monodimensional recasting of images and events but as an artwork as static and dynamic at once as any sculpture, as any architectural design; a literature in which the mind of the creative artist exists within the planes of creativity and aesthetic structure that give import and significance to the work. Debates about the place of minimalism within the mimetic tradition are often reduced to analogies or metaphors. The issue is stated: can literature as the mirror of social reality (the classic mimetic metaphor) fold in upon itself and become another mirror reflecting both artistic processes and social realities in the more complex fashion of art as counterpoint to reality, and can the new "Mobius strip" perspective of minimalist art establish the "window on the world" that Joan Didion envisions as both the essence and the phenomenological achievement of minimalist art?

The true mimetic critic believes that the mirror must remain static, imposed, and moral (in Gardner's sense) and rejects the concept of the interplay between art and reality as multidimensional and complementary mirrors that the minimalist author proposes. The minimalist author, on the other hand, rejects the traditional mimetic view of art imitating reality in stasis as too limiting and too far removed from the realities of a technetronic society and proposes, instead, a metaphor for art and reality that captures the indeterminacy and philosophical relativism of life in the contemporary era. It is apparent that, in proposing a new understanding of the relationship of artistic to social processes, the minimalist author is both redefining a tradition and seeking a new ground of understanding from critics who must interpret and evaluate the minimalist author's work within the context of previous traditions and in consideration of the values and epistemologies in art that are considered to be universal.

A Cultic Voice

Ann Beattie's fiction has been caught up within the controversies that attend redefining the mimetic tradition to include or exclude minimalism, and assessments of her writing have been affected by the paradigmatic shift contemporary criticism is presently undergoing. Perhaps the most crippling onslaught on Beattie's fiction has come not from those who undervalue or fail to value at all the constructs of minimalist fiction, but from those critics who would dismiss Beattie as only "a cultic voice,"[23] a writer whose preoccupation with the mores of "the Woodstock generation" makes her work of minor historical significance only because her fascination with postsixties hippies vitiates the potentially universal import of her fiction.

Beattie admits herself that she has gotten very "hostile" to that response to her work:

I mean, people never say things like, "James Joyce, he was pretty mired in Dublin wasn't he? He really stayed pretty close to home, didn't he?" I mean, if that's what you have to say about Joyce, that's a pretty reductive approach to the work. And I feel the same way about my work. If people want to take that as a stepping stone for what I'm writing about, well, of course it's there. It's certainly true that people I write about are essentially my age, and so they were a certain age in the 60's and had certain common experiences and tend to listen to the same kind of music and get stoned and wear the same kind of clothes. I realize that it's all there, but what I've always hoped for is that somebody will then start talking more about the meat and bones of what I'm writing about.[24]

Beattie also makes it very clear that she does not consider herself (nor does she want to be perceived as) a social historian of her generation. "Reviewers were looking for an explanation of the sixties," she says. "They found the sixties as a touchstone in some of my stories and over-emphasized that aspect of the work. It's crazy. I don't think all of my characters have anything like the same attitude toward life. Some people seem to read my stories as though they were novels, as though all of these characters might get together at a large buffet." To the charge that her fiction does seem to focus upon a particular set of character types, Beattie responds: "I'd be the first to admit that I'm writing about a rather small, neurotic, overmonied, in some ways overprivileged and unhappy group of people, but I don't think this has anything to do with the sixties. Nor is this very prominent in my more recent work." Most famous writers—Hemingway, Fitzgerald, Faulkner—have "staked out a particular region and group of characters," Beattie indicates, in the effort to capture the universal significance of the particular aspects of a given period or of given character types. She adamantly does not see herself as detailing the moeurs of her generation with any less an eye toward universal aesthetic and philosophical significance than other writers in the realist tradition.[25] Yet she is also aware that no matter what her level of artistic achievement some critics will always choose to regard her as "a chronicler of the postlapsarian counterculture,"[26] even though, as she says, "I resist and resent being categorized as a spokesperson for the '60's."[27]

Certainly, Beattie's assessment of some critics' reactions to her work is an accurate one. In "Down and Out: The Stories of Ann Beattie," Joshua Gilder states of Beattie: "By some cabal of editors and critics . . . she has been designated the voice of her generation. A more cheerless voice it would be hard to imagine." Typifying the tendency many critics have to envision Beattie as merely a chronicler of her times, Gilder argues,

Beattie's staple characters are the dead-end kids of the Seventies and Eighties; born to privilege, they've in some curious way internalized the recession. They're not socially or economically blocked but psychologically burnt out; they drag themselves around her stories like worn sneakers sucking up the

mud of despair, making little squishy, sighing noises as they go. They listen
to Dylan records and think about the good old days and try to summon the
energy to roll a joint. Their lives hold no possibilities because, like the friends
sitting around a Columbus Avenue apartment in *Falling in Place,* they're simply too *wrecked* to order out for pizza.[28]

Acknowledging that Beattie does draw "a fairly accurate picture of a
certain sort of lost, counterculture wastrel," Gilder argues, nonetheless, Beattie's fiction "begs the question of the distinction between
literature and journalism" because "Beattie's listless writing replicates
in prose the affectless inner life of her characters, people who do their
best with Valium and pot to anesthetize their emotions and scramble
their brains."[29]

The case Gilder makes against Beattie's fiction is an interesting one
to consider because his views are highly representative of those who
condemn Beattie's writings largely because they find her character
types not to their liking. Gilder's negative critique only tangentially
considers issues of style, technique, aesthetic perspective, theme, or
structure in Beattie's fiction; essentially his review is directed toward
considering as not a fit subject for art the types of characters Beattie is
interested in portraying. Beattie's fictive universe, in other words, is
not the type of universe Gilder enjoys inhabiting; therefore, it follows
(in Gilder's mind) that the problem resides not in Gilder's perspective
but in the artistry of Beattie herself. Such a philosophical position
reduces the criticizing of art to a matter of taste, or personal preference,
rather than to one of aesthetic judgment, and Gilder's biases are revealed in his assertion that Beattie is a writer undeserving of the reputation she has attained because her works are not "enlightened by a
belief in the redemptive powers of art." "The one thing that her fiction
says loud and clear," Gilder argues, "is that there is no redemption
from despair and hopelessness, especially not in art."[30]

Gilder's assessment of Beattie's fiction is an interesting blend of the
critical stance that art should uplift the populace and the "anti-cultic
voice" position that Beattie's characters are inherently not worth portraying because their values and their ways of coping with reality are
different from those of the prevailing culture. The people who inhabit
"Beattieland" to Gilder are "Beattie-oids" and thus are not deserving
subjects of artistic portrayal or investigation. He would prefer that
Beattie take her "resigned pessimism" somewhere else than the literary
arena, which is reserved for artists like John Updike and John Cheever,
whom Gilder admires for their belief in art's redemptive powers.[31]

The appraisal Gilder makes of Beattie's fiction is vitiated by the fact that it lacks balance; numerous respected critics of contemporary literature have found much to praise in Beattie's work, yet Gilder finds nothing. Further, he seems to be establishing Beattie as a straw figure against which to attack and vent his spleen for what he perceives as a declining interest by contemporary authors in the value of moral art and the moral perspective in literature. Though it is easy to find flaws and deficiencies in the argument Gilder makes, perhaps the best redress to his negative critique resides in analyzing Beattie's fiction itself to see if the charges Gilder makes are valid or distorted. Toward that end, the best place to begin is at the beginning, with an analysis of Ann Beattie's first volume of short stories, *Distortions*.

Chapter Three
Distortions: The Early Fiction

Distortions, Ann Beattie's first volume of short stories, was published in 1976. At the time, the prevailing mode of postmodernism had largely run its course, all its literary experiments had been tried, all the rebellions against the constraints of traditional mimetic fiction undertaken, and all the ways of looking at the "story-shaped world" of postmodernist aesthetics established.[1] In Ann Beattie's opinion, and in the opinion of many critics, the literary world was ripe for a return to realism, even if that realism was mediated through postmodernist influences.[2] It was a time, too, in which the literary and social worlds were both interested in understanding the decade of the 1960s in American culture, a decade of individualism, social rebellion, and romanticism wedged between the halcyon conformity of the Eisenhower era and the frenetic materialism of the 1970s. It was a time in which, as Ann Beattie states, people were and continued to be "tremendously interested in either fancifying or romanticizing the 1960's." A conflux of events served to establish Beattie's reputation as an important literary newcomer: she was a neorealist in an era interested in a return to literary realism; she was, as she describes it, "a writer of a romantic period" that people were interested in learning more about,[3] and she was, by all accounts, a highly talented writer whose first volume of stories revealed a unique style and a keen awareness of human motivations.

"Dwarf House"

"Dwarf House," the first story in *Distortions,* opens with a question: "Are you happy? Because if you're happy I'll leave you alone."[4]

The question is a key one, for all the stories in the volume focus upon happiness and the distortions of perception, need, and self-deceit that make the search for happiness frustrated and incomplete. If one central theme unites the stories, it is that the pursuit of happiness is the most elusive and complex of human quests and yet also the most highly valued.

20

The question about happiness is posed by MacDonald to his brother James. MacDonald has been sent by his mother to ask James to leave the "dwarf house" he shares with several other dwarfs and return home. When James refuses, MacDonald responds that he needs to reassure their mother that James is happy.

"Tell her I'm as happy as she is."
"You know she's not happy."
"She knows I'm not, too. Why does she keep sending you?"
"She's concerned about you. She'd like you to live at home. She'd come herself . . . "
"I know. But she gets nervous around freaks." (15)

James tells MacDonald that he is in love with a woman who lives in the "dwarf house" and that he intends to marry her. MacDonald is deeply distressed and knows that the news will throw their mother into a paroxysm of self-pity and despair.

Three houses or "families" shape the thematic import of "Dwarf House," each representing different social and personal definitions of happiness. The first is the mother's house, which is described in distinctly unhappy terms as being closed-off, dark, and isolated. The mother is immersed emotionally in her sorrows over James's deformity. She is filled with self-pity that such a terrible tragedy as to be the mother of a dwarf could be imposed upon her by fate. Yet, she wants James to return and live with her because loneliness is a worse state of unhappiness than living daily with James and facing the fact of his handicap, a paradoxical perspective that makes her more histrionically and self-destructively "unhappy."

The second house is the "dwarf house" itself, inhabited by a group of dwarfs and one giant. In the "dwarf house," a true spirit of camaraderie, loyalty, and family exists. The dwarfs and the giant are bound together by an appreciation of their role as outcasts and "freaks," and their knowledge of their state gives them a type of existential freedom. Since they can never fit into society's definition of "happiness," they are free to pursue their own. They are existentially free to choose self-definition, because they have abandoned all illusions that they will ever find "happiness" in the conventional sense of the word.

The middle zone between the self-centered and self-reflexive "happiness" of the mother and the existentially defined freedom of the "dwarf house" is conventional reality, the house occupied by MacDonald. MacDonald is essentially a passive observer of the types of "happiness" he sees in his mother's house and in the "dwarf house." He is aware that he really belongs in neither realm, yet he is unable to formulate a definition of his own.

MacDonald often calls his wife from work to tell her that he is going to be tied up in a meeting for several hours and will be late coming home, but the phone call is a practiced and regular deception. At least once a week, MacDonald goes to a run-down bar across town. On one occasion, he asks his secretary Betty to come along with him. As they drive to the bar, MacDonald asks Betty her age, and she responds that she is thirty. He asks her how she can be thirty years old and not be a cynic yet. Betty replies, "Actually, if I didn't take two kinds of pills, I couldn't smile every morning and evening for you" (20).

When they arrive at the bar, MacDonald tells Betty,

> "If you don't feel like smiling, don't smile."
> "Then all the pills would be for nothing."
> "Everything is for nothing," he says.
> "If you weren't drinking, you could take one of the pills," Betty says. "Then you wouldn't feel that way." (20–21)

In the story's denouement, MacDonald, his wife, and his mother "stand amid a cluster of dwarfs and one giant" waiting for James's wedding to begin (22). The couple is married on the lawn outside the church. When the ceremony is over, James kisses the bride and the dwarfs swarm around them. "MacDonald thinks of a piece of Hershey bar he dropped in the woods once on a camping trip, and how the ants were all over it before he finished lacing his boot" (22–23). MacDonald steps forward to congratulate the couple, and he "sees that the bride is smiling beautifully—a smile no pills could produce—and that the sun is shining on her hair so that it sparkles. She looks small, and bright, and so lovely that MacDonald, on his knees to kiss her, doesn't want to get up" (23).

The ending of "Dwarf House" is characteristic of the type of "miniaturized epiphanies" that Gilder sees adorning Beattie's fiction. Beattie has described her endings as "elliptical"[5] and has commented that her endings are "very important" to her—much more important than beginnings."[6]

The image of the Hershey candy bar with the ants swarming over it, symbolic of hunger and of human need, is a classic example of a "miniaturized epiphany" in which large insights into human nature are revealed through small, almost trivial, gestures and events. The people at the wedding are so desperate for "happiness" that wherever they encounter it, in whatever form, they descend upon it, trying to devour whatever little piece they can find. This same theme is recapitulated in the image of MacDonald on his knees staring into the bride's face and being mesmerized by her smile of radiant, true happiness. MacDonald is literally hungry for the type of joy that the bride and James possess, and, as he stares into the bride's face in a moment of longing and loneliness, he wishes to possess a bit of the happiness the couple has found.

The ending of the story is not only effective as the symbolic and thematic keel of the story but for embodying what Jay Parini views as the most carefully developed and aesthetically significant aspect of Beattie's writings: "As always in Beattie's fiction, the real story takes place at the edge of what is shown. Her statements are really questions. And she poses hard questions for her readers about human relations, about what will suffice to make us happy."[7] At the edge of "Dwarf House," the reader is left to ponder the silence that surrounds the moment of insight and to wonder what type of "happiness" will be available to MacDonald now that he has glimpsed true happiness in the bride's beatific look of love and total self-acceptance.

"Snakes' Shoes"

"Snakes' Shoes" is another fictive universe in which "the real story takes place at the edge of what is shown." It focuses upon the emotional permutations involved in the relationships between Sam, his brother Richard, and Richard's ex-wife, Alice.

The story opens with the trio sitting on a rock in the middle of Hall's Pond, an image perhaps suggestive of the distance and isolation the three share—although Ann Beattie has stated that she likes "to bury things too obviously symbolic" in her stories.[8]

Richard, Sam, and Alice have agreed to get together again, at Sam's suggestion. To the meeting, Alice brings her ten-month-old baby from her second marriage and her daughter from her marriage with Richard. The little girl is never identified by name, nor is her age specifically given.

When the little girl notices a snake crawl out from a crack between two rocks on the shore, Sam, her uncle, tells her how snakes tuck their tails into their mouths and turn into hoops so they can roll down hill more easily.

"Why don't they just walk?" [the child asks].

"They don't have feet. See?" [Sam says].

At Alice's urging to tell the child the truth, Sam responds, "They have feet, but they shed them in the summer. If you ever see tiny shoes in the woods, they belong to the snakes."

"Tell her the truth," [Alice says again].

"Imagination is better than reality," [Sam says to the little girl]. (26)

There is a strong emphasis in the story upon Sam's statement that "imagination is better than reality." In fact, there is the suggestion that imagination is all that enables humans to endure the vagaries of life and especially the vagaries of human relationships.

When Richard and Alice were engaged, Sam had tried to talk Richard out of the marriage; his intense conviction was based upon not wanting to see Richard dominated by a wife in the same fashion that he was controlled by his mother and regimented out of his identity in the Air Force. The wedding takes place, however, and Richard and Alice invite Sam to spend the summer with them. He is so impressed with the love and devotion the two express to each other that he continues to return for part of each summer and for every Thanksgiving thereafter. Just as he is convinced that "everything was perfect" (28), Richard tells him that he and Alice are getting a divorce.

Sam has admired Alice for her patience, for the way in which she appears not to hold a grudge against her husband for burning a hole in an armchair or for tearing the mainsail on their sailboat (done by irresponsibly going out on the lake in a storm). But when he talks to Alice about the breakup, Alice says of Richard, "He burns up all the furniture. He acts like a madman with that boat. He's swamped her three times this year. I've been seeing someone else" (28).

Sam takes Richard to a bar to sympathize with him about Alice's affair with Hans, her German lover. Richard knows about Hans and seems to be more troubled by the fact that Hans is German than by the fact that Alice has taken a lover.

After much urging from Richard, Sam agrees to let Richard move in with him in New York, and Richard proceeds to turn Sam's apartment into a menagerie, filling it with a dog, a cat, a parakeet, and a rabbit. When the rabbit contracts a fever, it costs Sam one hundred sixty dollars to treat the animal's illness because Richard is unemployed and cannot pay for anything.

Sam keeps a record book of the debts that Richard owes him. In it he writes, "Death of rabbit—$160 to vet." When Richard does get a job, he looks over the debt book and goes into a rage at what Sam has done.

"Why couldn't you have just written down the sum?" he asks Sam. "Why did you want to remind me about the rabbit?" The incident so upsets Richard that he misses the second day on his job. "That was inhuman," he says to Sam. "'Death of rabbit—$160'—that was horrible. The poor rabbit. God damn you." Sam's perception is that Richard "couldn't get control of himself" (30–31).

Sam hears from Alice when his mother dies. It is an odd letter of condolence, and it seems to Sam that Alice is not very happy. Sam writes her a long letter saying that they should all get together. He knows of a motel out in the country where they can stay, perhaps for the weekend. Alice agrees to the idea, and the trio meet to stay at the same hotel but in different rooms. One afternoon, out on the rock in the pond, the "family" is again reunited, and the little girl asks Sam to tell her a story. Sam responds that he cannot think of one, noticing that the girl "had bony knees" and "was not going to be as pretty as her mother" (32). Richard asks Alice why she married Hans, and she replies, "I don't know why I married either of you" (33). Perhaps sensing the tension mounting between the couple, Sam offers to take the girl for a walk. He takes her hand, this time observing that "the little girl's knees stuck out. Sam felt sorry for her. He lifted her on his shoulders and cupped his hands over her knees so he wouldn't have to look at them" (33).

That evening, the "family" once more returns to the rock. The little girl, recalling a previous scene in which she had looked through a man's binoculars, says she wishes she could look through them again. "Here," Sam says, making two circles with the thumb and first finger of each hand. "Look through these" (29). The little girl leans over and looks up at the trees through Sam's fingers. "Much clearer, huh?" Sam says. The little girl is enjoying the game. "Let me see," Richard says, and looks through his brother's fingers. "Don't forget me," Alice says as she leans across Richard to "peer through the circles" (34). As Alice leans across him, Richard kisses the back of her neck, and the story closes.

The ending of the story provides not only another of the "miniaturized epiphanies" that characterize and define Beattie's fiction but a simultaneous union of the concept of vision and illusion. Certainly, the ending forces the reader to discover that what goes on at the surface in human action and in human relationships is not the full or even the clear picture. On the surface, Alice and Richard act the politest of ex-spouses; their marriage is in the past, and they are moving on to form and to share a friendship. Richard helps to take care of Alice's son by Hans, and Alice is cooperative in carrying out the suggestions and requests for the weekend that both Richard and Sam present. As the ending of the story indicates, however, Richard's emotions have not fallen so easily into social politeness and group cooperation. His kiss on Alice's neck is one of tenderness, perhaps, perhaps one of sadness or desire. It is both ironic and intriguing that the kiss takes place only within the illusory security of distorted vision—as the couple peers through the imaginary binoculars made by Sam's fingers and pretends to see something not actually seen. Only in this moment of distorted perception, of perception distorted toward the realm of fantasy, can Richard's real feelings surface.

Earlier in the story, Sam has tried to coax the little girl into believing that he wrote *Alice in Wonderland,* and perhaps no finer metaphor exists for the thematic dimensions of "Snakes' Shoes" than an allusion to a child's fairy tale about perception and insight—about the looking glass and its magical powers to distort reality and, in those distortions, reveal more truths than otherwise could be found. Through the looking glass, Richard and Alice discover truths about themselves and their feelings, and those truths, one hopes, are ultimately freeing. In "Snakes' Shoes," however, as in "Dwarf House," much of the power of the story takes place in the suggestive silence that surrounds the story's end. The reader can only wonder in "Dwarf House" what MacDonald will see or refuse to see once the spell of looking into the bride's face is broken. Similarly, the reader can only wonder or imagine what Richard and Alice, perhaps even Sam, will see once the protective circle of the imaginary looking glass is withdrawn and reality must be seen in a different light, a different focus.

"The Parking Lot"

Adulterous affairs and the romantic illusions associated with pas-sionate, sexual love seem to be the predominant mode of escapism in *Distortions.* Characters search for the love they do not possess by in-volving themselves in temporary liaisons they know will not keep them secure (or even desired) for long. The romances and attractions seem to be only temporary stays against confusion, distractions from the deeper pain of these characters' lives; but the characters find their real lives to be even more emotionally unfulfilled than the fantasies they pursue.

In "The Parking Lot," a couple's marriage is shown to be an empty series of domestic rituals centering upon food and its preparation. The woman, who is never named, works in an office building surrounded by a vast parking lot. Throughout the story, the parking lot itself becomes a metaphor for the work place—vast, empty, demarcated, never-changing—a place in which the woman can lose herself and not have to face the larger and more real loss of her own identity. Each time she walks across the parking lot, she becomes fascinated by "the sameness of the surface: so black and regular" (188), yet, the same regularity and "sameness of the surface" associated with her marriage begin to feel isolating and deadening to her.

The woman has an arrangement with her husband, Jim; they alternate the years in which they work. Last year, he worked as a house painter; this year, she has an office job. They survive, too, by sharing not only the economic responsibilities of the marriage but the domestic responsibilities as well. Jim does all the grocery shopping, and the woman is a superb cook, consistently preparing gourmet meals of exotic combinations.

During the day, Jim searches for spices and herbs and whatever delicacies his wife might need that evening, while the woman immerses herself in her work at the office. "Only work has seemed real to her since she began her job"; "the wide, shining hallway gives her a sense of purpose" (189).

The couple has a friend, Sam, who often comes to visit them. Sam is separated from his wife and seems to come to the couple's home for a vicarious sense of participating in marriage and in a domestic routine. Sam and Jim often go out together and invite the woman to go along with them, but she declines. "When they leave the apartment it seems suddenly as though space is opening up around her" (190).

The woman is aware that "Sam has always been a little in love with her," and she "likes him a little more because she knows about his secret love" (191). But she also feels uncomfortable around Sam because his presence is "a reminder of what can happen to a marriage, the distressing realization that two adults who care about each other as Sam and his wife do, can't reach some agreement, have some arrangement that will make them both happy" (192).

One day, the woman is walking from work toward her car in the parking lot, and a car pulls up along side of her. She recognizes the

driver as "a man she has spoken to several times in the elevator" (192).
He asks her if she is parked in the back of the lot and offers her a ride.
She gets in, and they are at her car in less than a minute—" 'too short
a time to start a conversation,' he says" (192). She agrees and remains
in the car for awhile longer. "She smiles, which is something she hasn't
done all weekend" (192). "During the next hour they have a conversation—in a bar. The conversation lasts about an hour, and then they
go to a motel and go to bed. She thinks, then, of Jim—as she has most
of the afternoon. She cannot decide what to tell him, so she stays in
the motel for another hour, thinking. Eventually they leave. He drives
her back to her car. They smile again. This time there is no conversation, and she gets out" (192–93).

The next day she does not go to work but loses herself in a shopping
spree in a department store, buying expensive perfume, and in making
an elaborate meal for Jim. The following day she returns to work and
expects that the man "will be in her office waiting for her, but she
doesn't see him all that day" (194). At the day's close, she leaves work,
crosses the parking lot, and then she sees his car. She approaches the
car, and, for a moment, stands with her hand against the window
"until he reaches across the seat and opens the door on her side. Then
she gets into the car" (194–95).

The woman knows that eventually her husband will find out. One
evening she is particularly late and had delayed calling for hours. She
uses the phone at the entrance to the parking lot, trying to keep her
voice calm and regular. She counts the white lines that divide the lot
into parking places until Jim answers. She tells him that her car has
broken down and that there is a man there who will help her. Jim
listens and asks several questions; then there is silence. He tells her to
call him if there is any real trouble.

The man drives her to her car at the back of the lot. She watches in
the rearview mirror as his car drives away, and then she gets out of her
car and stands in the parking lot. "Standing there, she thinks of her
lover, gone in one direction, and of Jim, in another." Then "she gets
in the car and drives home to make dinner" (196).

"The Parking Lot" is an interesting study in loneliness. The woman
feels confined by her marriage and her life. Her work, which exhausts
her by the end of the day, also frees her because it provides her a reason
to be away from home and to immerse herself in another perspective,
another environment. For love and real communication, she and her
husband have substituted cooking and eating rituals, perhaps in an

attempt to fill themselves physically in ways they cannot emotionally. The emotional bankruptcy of their marriage makes the woman seek a type of fulfillment through an affair with a coworker.

One might wonder why the woman does not become involved with Sam since he loves her, and she is attracted both to Sam and to his admiration of her. Yet, it is apparent from the story's context that Sam represents the reality of a failed union, of the inability of love and marriage to conquer all and to survive. This is a realization that the woman is not yet ready to face in her own life. She clings to the hope that she can find emotional fulfillment by losing herself in a sexual involvement that does not even attempt or pretend to involve love or commitment. In this distraction, she pulls herself away from her marriage, which has become a phantasm of unexpressed and unfulfilled emotions.

Because reality is too harsh and the awareness that love does not conquer all too difficult to accept at this point in her life, the woman substitutes the temporary self-deception that an affair with a virtual stranger will at least free her from some of the emotional pain and alienation she feels. Her pursuit of emotional wholeness and fulfillment is a quest fostered by resignation and despair and sustained by illusion. The woman is aware that her marriage has not become the type of union she desires; yet, rather than accept this realization and its implications for personal growth and change, she endeavors to let a chance encounter in the parking lot outside her office building alchemize her life. When reality cannot be accepted and vision cannot be joined with action, escapism remains the only option, and, for Beattie's characters, escapism is often only the visible expression of failed attempts at meaningful self-definition.

"Imagined Scenes"

Like "The Parking Lot," "Imagined Scenes" addresses the themes of loneliness, longing, and frustrated love, but this time measured and assessed against the themes of old age and loss. The life and emotional interaction of a married couple, David and his wife (who remains unnamed throughout the story) are examined in contrast to the life of an elderly widower; the loneliness of the old man serves as a symbolic comment upon the emotional drift and distancing David and his wife undergo.

The story opens with a note of emotional intensity between the couple but also with suggestions of the compromises their relationship has exacted. The woman is dreaming of a trip to Greece and awakens to share her excitement with her husband. David is awake already, and she remembers a time the previous year, the week before Christmas, when they had both come home with their purchases. She was at the front door struggling with her keys when David drove up. He jumped out of the car, excited about his purchases, and reached around to put his key in the lock for her. "Now she expects him to wake up when she does, that they will arrive home simultaneously" (54). But her husband still surprises her. At the end of the summer he had told her that he would not return to work but would be going back to school to finish his Ph.D.

Since that decision, their life had become, in part, a series of unspoken compromises, manifested as rituals. He sits in a chair by the fireplace and reads; she brings coffee to the table by his chair. When she is tired, he turns off the lights and goes upstairs with her to bed. "By unspoken agreement, he has learned to like Roquefort dressing" (54), and he pokes the logs in the fireplace for her because she is afraid of the hot red coals.

The woman works at night. She is a nurse and has been hired by an old man's daughter and son-in-law to stay with him at night for a week while they are out of town. His sister is to stay with him during the days.

One afternoon, the woman returns home early from work and finds that David has gone for a walk with the dog. Company has been in the house. She finds coffee cups, spoons, and forks scattered about the kitchen and an apple pie she does not remember buying. When David comes in, he tells her that he has met the people who moved in down the hill, Katherine and Larry Duane. He has agreed to help them put in a sink, and, as he leaves to go back to the Duanes, he does not take the dog with him.

The next night, late in the evening, she looks at her watch to see if it is time to give the old man his medicine and discovers that her watch is not there. She calls David to find out if she has left her watch at home. She lets the phone ring a long time, but there is no answer.

The following night at work, she calls David at four in the morning. There is no answer. When the old man awakens, he can tell that she is very worried.

"I tried to get my husband last night but there was no answer."
"Men are heavy sleepers."
"No," she says. "He'd wake up." (60)

It is snowing heavily. The old man asks her to call his sister and tell her not to come. If anything happens, he can call. She phones the sister and gives her the message, but she is coming anyway. "It's terrible to be old," the old man says. "You have no power" (61).

David comes to get his wife, knowing that her car will never make it up the hill in the snow and sleet. They drive through the blinding snow, and the woman says to David, "I called you last night and there was no answer."

"You called?"
"Yes. You weren't there."
"I didn't know it was you. I was asleep. Why were you calling?"
"I guess you were walking the dog in the woods."
"I just told you, I was asleep." (62–63)

As they drive home, she closes her eyes and imagines a series of scenes about David: David sleeping; David playing with the dog, holding a branch high into the air for the dog to jump up to; David asleep again, under the covers; David walking up the hill. She tries to imagine more but is afraid that if she does not open her eyes she will fall asleep.

Back home, she closes her eyes again. The curtains are drawn, and the house is dark. David says he is going downstairs to clean up. The phone rings, and she comes downstairs to answer it. "The table is clear. Everything has been cleared away" (63).

It is the old man's sister on the phone. She is snowed in and cannot reach her husband. The old man's daughter and son-in-law cannot return. Their plane is grounded in Florida. The sister is asking if the woman can possibly come back and stay the night with the old man.

As she listens to the sister, the woman imagines the runway in Florida filling up with snow. No planes will land tonight, and no one is at home in the United States; "they're up in the air, above the snow" (64). She wonders what was on the table when she came in and notices that David has also cleaned up the room. "You're so lucky," the sister says to her. "You can come and go. You don't know what it's like to be caught" (64).

"Imagined Scenes" combines the triad of vision, imagination, and escapism that so largely determines Beattie's philosophical stance and the thematic structuring of her stories. The woman in "Imagined Scenes" goes through a variety of emotional stages representative of changes in her vision. As the story begins, she is lost in a dream. When she awakens, she retreats into memories of fond times in her life with David. Interacting with David, she believes that she sees him and their marriage clearly, envisioning David as impulsive and whimsical in his career choice, perhaps, but overall the epitome of devoted love. Her interaction with David indicates that she sees him as the center of her experience. She wants always to be with him—to awaken with him, to share enthusiastic and exciting moments with him, to help him attain his goals in his career. In her daily routine with David, she feels strongly that she knows him well and that the unspoken agreements they have made to give structure to their marriage have been positive and effective. In truth, however, as John Romano points out, "the daily schedules of the couple barely overlap. They do not inhabit the same hours, and there is something chilling and mysterious about the gap between them."[9]

The woman is more obviously attached to David than he is to her. She is only separated from David when he leaves her to take a walk, or to visit the Duanes, or when she goes to stay with the old man. In these moments with the old man, she must imagine David and recreate him in her mind. As the story progresses, she can find less and less refuge in fantasy and memory—in "imagined scenes"—and must face some very difficult and unsettling realities that necessitate a reshaping of her vision of her life with David.

In contrast to "The Parking Lot," the adultery in "Imagined Scenes" is only hinted at. As Romano indicates, the "frequent signs of inexplicable activity" (such as the coffee cups on the table and a favorite plant given away to the Duanes) combined with David's plausible though sketchy explanations "seem slightly sinister in the haze of mutual incomprehension. The glimpses, the physical data, which the woman has of her husband's life in her absence tell her nothing, though they hint at guilty secrets. They cannot be either ignored or interpreted."[10]

The fact that David is not home the two nights the woman calls, that he is reluctant to take his wife down to meet the Duanes, and that he is so obviously uncomfortable in discussing where he has been and what he has been doing in his wife's absence are key indications that he has most likely been involved in an affair. For David, perhaps, the adultery is an escape from the unspoken agreements by which he and his wife have structured their lives. Perhaps it is indicative of a certain loss of direction in his life, exemplified by his desire to complete his doctorate but his inability to get any academic work done during the course of the story.

As in many of Beattie's stories, the adultery is indicative of Beattie's belief that what is most significant in individual human lives and relationships occurs below the visible level of everyday existence. In "Imagined Scenes," the woman's subconscious mind—her memories and fantasies—are far more revealing of her true emotional state than her conscious mind. Similarly, David's adultery, which takes place "off stage" in the story and within the obscurity of night, is far more important and revealing than his daily and daytime interactions with his wife.

The great metaphor in the story for the encroachment of reality is the snow that falls until it finally traps everyone in a kind of nebulous inertia. The story begins with a dream of warmth on the summer beaches of Greece and ends with the snow immobilizing all the characters and freezing the entire city into a virtual standstill. From the warmth of their house, David goes out into the snow and meets the Duanes; his liaison with Katherine will eventually take away the warmth from his home and leave his wife feeling emotionally exhausted and trapped. It is in nights of heavy snow that the woman calls her house and discovers David's absences. In the worst storm of the winter, David and his wife drive home in angered, tense silence after the woman has discovered and admitted to herself David's infidelity, and the most poignant and thematically rich line of the story is presented. The radio in the car is turned on, and "the weather forecast calls for more snow" (63).

The snow that surrounds the town, the couple, their home, their lives, is emblematic of the slow and deep disillusionment that occurs in the story. The dream of Greece that began the story has become, by its end, a symbol of immobility and of unattainable fantasy. The woman must confront the painful loss of illusions in the same fashion that the old man must envision age as another threatening and immobilizing agent.

"It's terrible to be old. You have no power," the old man says (61).
Just as easily, the woman could state, "It's terrible to be disillusioned.
You have no power."

John Romano describes "Imagined Scenes" as a story that shows the
unique way in which Beattie makes her material her own. "We do not
realize, or not all at once, that what the young woman has 'imagined'
is not her husband's private or guilty activity. She has accepted not the
explanations but the sufficiency unto themselves of the physical facts.
She 'imagines' only that she is in Greece, or some place warm, by the
sea, while the scene of her actual present life is snowy. It is the reader
who has been seduced into guessing at the husband's hidden life." Romano sees "Imagined Scenes" as representative of Beattie's skill in the
short story genre.

We guess at the "real facts" of the woman's life because we care about her, her
sadness has been made significant. It follows that the author has cared about
her in the making. But then it is more astonishing to perceive that the woman
cares so little, so indistinctly, for herself. She is not suspicious, she has no
imagination; the mark of Beattie's respect for this creation is not to have
slipped her some healthy suspicion, as it were, under the counter. In this
forbearance the writer resembles some impossible ideal of a loving parent who
succeeds in not interfering in her children's lives. To love one's characters—
Tolstoy is the presiding genius here—is to allow them to be who they are.[11]

Countering those critics who attack Beattie for her dispassionate,
restrained, and seemingly aloof style, Romano argues that, in a Beattie
story, "only later does the sympathetic center of her work betray itself.
We may feel misled by the outward reserve, but, again, her willingness
to distort when necessary, her passion for the particular, is ultimately
an index of her concern for the integrity of things and people in
themselves."[12]

"Fancy Flights"

If one envisions "Snakes' Shoes" and "Imagined Scenes" as commen-
taries upon the theme of illusion versus reality, or, more specifically,
the theme of the imagination as a protection against the intrusion of
too much painful reality, it is interesting to view the story "Fancy
Flights" as a comment upon the total rejection of reality in favor of

the world of illusion, specifically a drug-induced flight away from the strictures and responsibilities of everyday social and personal interaction.

Much has been made of Beattie's focus upon drugs in her fiction and the illusory worlds that drugs generate for her characters. Joshua Gilder considers this focus "one reason why Beattie People never seem to do much of anything."[13] Gilder is particularly disturbed by the pervasive presence of marijuana, cocaine, and valium in Beattie's fiction, describing this aspect of her work as fiction operating in "the comatose mode." The presentation of characters so in need of escapism by such vacuous and self-destructive means is one more proof, Gilder contends, of Beattie's inability to deal ethically and realistically with human choice and freedom.[14]

Clearly, Beattie's fiction does include a strong emphasis upon characters who rely on drugs, and *Distortions* is no exception. It is a limiting critical notion, however, to regard the depiction of characters dependent upon chemical alterations of their perceptions of reality as indicative of Beattie's inability or refusal to write moral fiction. Rather, one should view Beattie as a neorealist whose faithfully realistic descriptions of life in the 1970s and 1980s must include depictions of drug use and drug dependency.

Like many of Beattie's fictions, "Fancy Flights" centers upon alienation and emotionally fractured lives. Michael, the central character, is separated from his wife, Elsa, and from his four-and-a-half-year-old daughter, Mary Anne. His deepest emotional bond, in fact, seems to be with his dog Silas, and his interaction with Silas is the story's opening motif.

Silas is afraid of vacuum cleaners, little children, and music, all of which he growls at, and "his growling always gets him in trouble; nobody thinks he is entitled to growl" (36). Silas gets extremely agitated at Bob Dylan's song "Positively Fourth Street," and Michael believes that "if the dog had his way, he would get Dylan by the leg in a dark alley" (36). He imagines that maybe he and Silas could take a trip to a recording studio or concert hall, "wherever Dylan was playing," and then "Silas could get him" (36). "Thoughts like these ('fancy flights,' his foreman called them) were responsible for Michael's no longer having a job" (36).

Michael had worked in a furniture factory. During his breaks, he smoked hash in the parking lot in the back of the factory. Often, dur-

ing his shifts, he would break into hysterical laughter at jokes his
fellow employees would tell. "Every day he smoked as much hash as
he could stand" (36).

Michael depends on his grandmother for support in the form of
"words of encouragement, mail-order delicacies, and money" (37). He
lives in a house that belongs to his friends Prudence and Richard, who
are in Manila. Michael is house-sitting for his friends and does not
have to pay rent, only the utility bills. He spends his days and evenings
listening to music, smoking hash, playing with Silas, and going
through Prudence's and Richard's bureau drawers. "He usually eats two
cans of Campbell's Vegetarian Vegetable soup for lunch and four
Chunky Pecan candy bars for dinner. If he is awake in time for break-
fast, he smokes hash" (38).

One day, Michael calls his wife. He learns that his daughter, Mary
Anne, is having trouble in the day-care center. Mary Anne wants to
quit, stay home, and watch television. His wife asks if Michael would
stay with Mary Anne during the day and let her have her wish, "since
her maladjustment is obviously caused by Michael's walking out on
them when he *knew* the child adored him" (41).

Michael says he called to say he was lonesome because Silas has run
away.

"I really love that dog," [Michael says].
"What about Mary Anne?" [Elsa asks].
"I don't know. I'd like to care, but what you said didn't make any impres-
sion on me." (42)

Michael has a friend named Carlos who amazes Michael because he
can cast curses upon people and objects and "roll a joint in fifteen
seconds" (43). Carlos speaks to Michael about the possibility of getting
a job in Carlos's father's factory. Michael tells him that he is through
with jobs and with all machinery and tells Carlos to put a curse on his
father's machines.

"What if I put a curse on you?" Carlos asks.
"I'm already cursed," Michael says, " . . . I myself am cursed with ill
luck." (44)

The next day, Silas returns home. Michael finds him standing in the
front yard. He takes Silas inside, hugs and pets him; then there is a
knock at the door. It is Michael's wife, Elsa, who tells him, "I've come

to get you and make you come home and share the responsibility for Mary Anne."

> "I don't want to come home," [Michael says].
> "I don't care. If you don't come home, we'll move in here."
> "Silas will kill you."
> "I know the dog doesn't like me, but he certainly won't kill me." (46)

Elsa tells Michael decisively to come home and help with Mary Anne, who is driving Elsa crazy. Michael gets Silas, his bag of grass and his pipe, and what remains of a bag of pecans his grandmother has sent him, and goes with Elsa.

> "I'm not asking you to work right away," [Elsa says]. I just want you in the house during the day with Mary Anne."
> "I don't want to hang around with her."
> "Well, you can fake it. She's your daughter."
> "I know. That doesn't make any impression on me."
> "I realize that," [Elsa says]. (47)

Michael spends his days taking care of Mary Anne and watching soap operas. One afternoon, Mary Anne and a friend are having an imaginary tea party. Carlos calls, and Michael asks him, "Why don't you cast a spell and make things better?" (50).

Michael "looks at his daughter and her friend enjoying their tea party" (50–51) and then goes into the bathroom, closes the door, and lights up his pipe. He sits on the bathroom floor with his legs crossed and gets very stoned. He can hear a woman crying on the soap opera. Mary Anne's pink plastic bunny stares at him from the bathtub. "'What else can I do?' he whispers to the bunny. He envies the bunny—the way it clutches the bar of soap to its chest" (51).

When Elsa returns, Michael goes into the hall and "puts his arms around her, thinking about the bunny and the soap. Mick Jagger sings to him: 'All the dreams we held so close seemed to all go up in smoke. . .'" (51).

> "Elsa," he says, "What are your dreams?"
> "That your dealer will die," she says.

He asks her to be serious and tell him "one real dream." "I told you," Elsa says (51).

Michael lets Elsa go and walks into the living room. He sees Carlos pull up and goes out and gets into Carlos's car. Michael is somber and noncommunicative, and his mood is "contagious." Carlos angrily starts the car and drives off, "throwing a curse on a boxwood at the edge of the lawn" (51).

While ostensibly a story about the impact of drug dependency upon Michael's life, "Fancy Flights" is, on a much deeper level, a story about loneliness and emotional suffering. Michael's drug use is only symptomatic of deeper emotional hurts and longings—the cumulative effect of which is to present a picture of a man unable to cope with his life or to function within it in a meaningful fashion.

Clearly, in his interpersonal relationships, Michael is capable of very little closeness or responsibility. He frees himself of anything that might place strictures upon his life or make demands upon his emotional energies—his wife, daughter, job, self-esteem, motivation, and capacity for inner-directed vision. In ridding himself of both his marriage and his job, Michael, in a sense, regresses to a type of adolescence (and a very childlike adolescence at that), staying home and getting stoned all day; refusing to work and letting his grandmother and his wife support him; eating soup and Chunky Pecan candies; playing with Silas as his only true companion or buddy—being, in essence, as free as possible from any of the responsibilities and implications of self-definition.

In his talks with Carlos, Michael blames his dysfunctional and apathetic state upon "ill luck" (44), failing (perhaps even refusing) to realize how many of his own problems and troubles he has brought upon himself. Like many adolescents, Michael blames his misfortunes and problems on others and remains happy as long as he can be self-indulgent and irresponsible. In his world of self-induced self-deception, he does not have to face up to the existential implications of personal freedom; instead, all Michael has to do is live in an imagined, euphoric world of "fancy flights."

Michael's adolescent refuge is violated and altered when his wife, Elsa, comes to take him home. The irony of his wife's coming for him as if he were a child who has misbehaved is surpassed only by the heavy parent-child interaction that Michael and Elsa engage in until the last scene of the story. Perhaps most significantly, the world that Elsa brings Michael into is that of a type of illusory childhood—he is to serve as a kind of playmate and companion for his four-and-a-half-year-old daughter, a role for which Michael seems ideally suited in terms of his own emotional immaturity, but one that he does not want because of the implied adult responsibilities caring for Mary Anne encompasses.

In the last scene of the story, Michael is forced into a painful realization of his emotional state and his lot in life. Watching his daughter having her tea party with her friend, knowing that his wife and even Carlos (with all his magic) are at work, Michael experiences a sense of displacement and alienation that is exceedingly painful, yet illuminating. Admiring with poignant longing the bond that his daughter and her friend share at the tea party, Michael goes into the bathroom to smoke pot, his usual custom and his usual way of dealing with both loneliness and painful emotions. Even here, in his drug-induced fantasies of a world protected from painful intrusions, he cannot escape the realization that even the plastic bunny, which functions as both a bath toy and a soap holder, has more purpose in life than he.

"What else can I do?" (51) he asks of the bunny, meaning that since Michael does not truly fit into the world of childhood represented by his daughter and her friend, or into the world of adulthood, represented by his wife and Carlos at work, what else can he do but get stoned and try to live in a world of delusions and self-imposed deceptions?

This time, however, the magic of the drugs to transport him away from adulthood and responsibility is not sufficient, and Michael is forced to face a measure of truth about his world and his life. He remembers a line from Mick Jagger's song "Angie," and, as he embraces his wife, he realizes that "all the dreams we held so close seemed to all go up in smoke . . . " (51), a clear indication that Michael is beginning to realize how much of his own state of dysfunction and apathy he has brought upon himself. His life and his dreams are going up in smoke, and he feels powerless to do anything about the dissipation he is experiencing. Rather than fight it, Michael chooses to leave his wife, and the clarity of vision she represents, to go off with Carlos, and to reidentify himself with the world of magic and drug-induced "fancy flights."

Gilder has stated that "perhaps the most telling of Beattie's emotional economies is her characters' inability to muster the energy to pass beyond adolescence. Their limit to growth is about age eighteen, which among other things explains their nostalgia for the Sixties, when the whole culture seemed to have regressed into adolescence."[15] While "Fancy Flights" is indeed a story about one character's "inability to muster the energy to pass beyond adolescence," it is also a story representative of failings in human character and relationships. The weaknesses that Michael reveals are emblematic of personal failings that are generated by a preference for refuge and security, however illusory, over the terrifying implications of taking responsibility for one's own life. In this regard, Beattie is less a writer depicting a certain character type of the "lost, counterculture wastrel" than she is a writer revealing deep insights into the nature of the human psyche and the human will.

Darkness and Light

Peter Glassman has commented that, in assembling in *Distortions* a "bizarre collection of the lonely, the disoriented, and the dispossessed," Beattie has achieved a "measure of consummate technical virtuosity." Beattie's "frigid prose, the shocking inexorableness of her humor and narrative designs, the macabre and spare efficiency of her thought, conspire to project her tales as actual—if rather awful—occurrences of modern existence."[16] Glassman is aware that, in contrast to many contemporary writers, Beattie does not assume an ironic distance from her characters, which might make their sufferings and conundrums seem like parodies of contemporary life. Instead, "Beattie constructs her stories from within a soft and subtle sensibility of sympathy, participation, and hopefulness. She understands that, however capricious or queer, her characters' pains have their origin less in the morasses of individual neurosis than in the insipidity of the culture at large, the withering vapidity of the historical processes which envelop one and with which one must manage to coexist in some sort of emotional relation." The collapse of characters' inner lives is but a reflection of the spiritually bankrupt world in which they live, for Beattie comprehends, in Glassman's opinion, "that we are driven into our misery and peculiarity because, appropriately, we cannot accommodate the abstraction and absurdity which surround us."[17]

Larry Husten, in considering both the merit and philosophical implications of *Distortions*, envisions Beattie as "a sharp cultural observer" who "focuses on the interaction between her characters and their culture." In Husten's view, those of Beattie's characters "who abandon their selves to the cultural moment lose the ability to experience genuine emotion."[18] Husten's construct for Beattie's philosophical dichotomy of will and apathy, feeling and emptiness, is the metaphor of darkness and light that he says pervades Beattie's fictive universe in *Distortions*. Characters who are lost in their culture's mazes of emotional and spiritual entropy are often identified with the dark; other characters, who deny the sterility and the penchant for self-annihilation in the modern world, "retain a core of self and the ability to feel."[19] For these characters, who struggle for self-definition, light, in the form of self-insight and the will to self-determination, is their bounty. As Husten states, all Beattie's characters in *Distortions* "face, or will face, the darkness. What makes Beattie so interesting and popular a writer . . . is not *her* response to this darkness (by now a trite concept) but the ways in which she imagines her characters' responses."[20]

For characters like MacDonald, facing the darkness and the silence while staring into the light in the bride's face in "Dwarf House," or the wife in "Imagined Scenes," watching the snow falling and immersing her life in darkness and freezing cold, the light of existential self-definition is still a possibility. That some, like Michael in "Fancy Flights," allow their lives and dreams to go up in smoke, or others, like the wife in "The Parking Lot," wait for circumstances to overwhelm them and force change upon them, does not negate that the light, the other choice that might have been made, waits (like the silence) at the edge of Beattie's fictional world. Were the choices between darkness and light clear-cut and easy for her characters, Beattie would be the type of moral writer with ready ethical and existential answers that Gilder and many other critics admire. As it is, Beattie is concerned with defining a universe of distortions, of fluctuations in darkness and light, that make the choices seem more ambiguous, more obscure. Through these distortions, Beattie depicts not only the essences of her characters' lives but presents powerful insights into the patterns of contemporary life.

Chapter Four
Chilly Scenes of Winter

"Chilly Scenes"

Ann Beattie's formal literary debut as an author of books was both unique and impressive, with Doubleday simultaneously publishing her first novel, *Chilly Scenes of Winter*, and her first volume of short stories, *Distortions*, on 13 August 1976. The move was designed by the publisher to draw attention to Beattie as a new talent, and it proved an extremely effective technique.[1] *Chilly Scenes of Winter* was offered as a Book-of-the-Month Club alternate, and reviewers who critiqued Beattie's achievement generally responded to both works in their assessments.

While the critical response to *Distortions* was generally favorable, though somewhat mixed, the response to *Chilly Scenes of Winter* was almost universally laudatory. Beattie was praised as a mesmerizing and unique literary talent, and *Chilly Scenes of Winter* was compared to J. D. Salinger's *Catcher in the Rye* for capturing and distilling the mood of the 1970s as Salinger's novel had etched into literary memory the atmosphere of the 1950s.[2]

In essence, *Chilly Scenes of Winter* is a love story, played out against scenes of the 1970s in America. Benjamin DeMott in *Surviving the 70's* describes the decade as unique, for, following on the heels of the highly idealistic and ideologically defined 1960s, it was the first era to substitute trends and fads for personal and cultural mythologies. DeMott sees the *The Whole Earth Catalogue*, the archetypal icon and the Bible of the seventies, as indicative of the era's values and perspectives—a type of "mod wishbook" in which all trendy fantasies could be satisfied and the earth itself could be contained within faddish categories and hip definitions.[3]

One may think of *Chilly Scenes of Winter* as a type of "mod wishbook" on love in the seventies, for the novel explores and satirizes many of the clichés of romantic love dominant at the time, and most of the characters of *Chilly Scenes of Winter* are known more by their wishes or fantasies than by what they actually do with their lives.

The central character in the novel is Charles, who is in love with Laura, a married woman who lives in an A-frame house, bakes bread, and cares for her husband, Jim, and her stepdaughter Rebecca. Laura is alternately envisioned by Charles as a symbol of settled, domestic bliss or of an exotic romantic life freed from social restraints and petty bourgeois considerations. Laura has come to mean so much to Charles, to have taken on so much significance in his personal life, that he is literally obsessed with her and with his desire to win her away from Jim and to have her love forever.

Charles's quest for Laura's love is by turns comic and pathetic and is enacted amidst the emotional chaos of Charles's relationship to his own family, who represent, metaphorically, another perspective on love and marriage. Charles's mother, Clara, is a self-centered neurotic given to histrionics and hypochondria. She regularly calls Charles and his sister Susan at odd hours to come and minister to her imagined physical woes. Clara is convinced that she is dying and that her children do not care about her because they do not take an interest in her sufferings. Susan tends to view Clara's sufferings as genuine, though somewhat overly dramatized; Charles, however, views his mother's theatrics as both manipulations and existential statements. "If you want to know what I really think," he says to Susan, "I think that one day she just decided to go nuts because that was easier. This way she can say whatever she wants to say, and she can drink and lie around naked and just not do anything."[4]

Clara is married to Pete, her second husband. Her first husband, Charles and Susan's father, died at thirty-nine and is perceived by both Clara and his children as a model of virtue and understanding. Pete, on the other hand, is intensely disliked by Charles and only moderately tolerated by Susan—largely because she feels sorry for him and does not want to add any additional pressures on her mother's delicate emotional condition. Pete openly seeks Charles's and Susan's attention and love and becomes even more obnoxious to them by constantly pressuring them to admit that they dislike him and then endeavoring to manipulate them into loving him out of a sense of guilt and responsibility.

While Susan is generally tolerant and patient with Pete, attributing his demanding nature to insecurities and the pressures of living with Clara, Charles dismisses Pete as an eccentric loser who is incapable of seeing Clara (and therefore his marriage to Clara) clearly. Charles describes Pete as "a grown man with a messed-up wife" (78) who refuses to face the reality of his situation by making up comfortable fantasies about Clara and then trying to foist them off on others. When Clara is confined to a hospital for what she claims is an appendicitis attack, Pete tries to minimize the incident by telling both Charles and Susan that "Mommy" (as Pete calls Clara) is prone to exaggeration. When "Mommy" goes into the bathroom and swallows twelve laxative tablets because no one will believe she is really sick, Pete claims that the doctors do not understand her. Finally, when "Mommy" is placed in a mental hospital because of her increasingly aberrant behavior, Pete's solution is to enroll them both in a Fred Astaire dancing class so that "Mommy" will have something to take her mind off her troubles.

One of the most effective ironies of *Chilly Scenes of Winter* is that Charles is exceedingly hostile toward Pete because he envisions Pete as a fool for being unable to recognize Clara for what she is—in other words, for being unable to see clearly and realistically the woman he loves. Yet, this failure to perceive one's beloved clearly is exactly the malady Charles suffers from in the exaggerated and highly romanticized notions of Laura that he maintains throughout the novel, despite much realistic evidence to the contrary. Thematically, it is an interesting twist in the novel that Charles, who thinks he is insightful because he can see the absurdities of Pete's distorted perceptions of Clara, is guilty of the same misperceptions generated by obsessive love.

Images of marriage in *Chilly Scenes of Winter* are generally negative. Pete and Clara's marriage is portrayed as a maze of twisted emotional needs predicated upon neuroses and a distorted sense of reality. Jim and Laura's marriage is shown to be emotionally vacuous and compromised by Laura's adultery with Charles. One couple, whom Charles knows only vaguely, sends him a Christmas card in which the wife details the husband's adulterous affair with a younger woman and the couple's reconciliation, which is due to the fact that the younger woman kicked the husband out after only a short time. "It's nuts to get married," Sam, Charles's best friend, says. "What would you get married for?" (65), summing up the prevailing motif in the novel that marriage is both a pointless and a perilous venture.

In the thematic design of the novel, Sam serves as an effective contrast to Charles. The two have been friends since childhood, and Charles admits to worshipping Sam because he sees him as everything that Charles is not. Sam "always has great success with women" (2), while Charles is an admitted failure. Sam's self-confidence is matched by Charles's self-doubt, and, while Sam is able to avoid all deep emotional involvements and commitments, Charles falls deeply in love with Laura and cannot free himself from her memory. In many ways, Sam is the contemporary image of youth in the 1970s. He is a college graduate, a member of Phi Beta Kappa, who works as a clothing salesman because he does not have the motivation to go to law school. His romantic involvements are short-term and based solely upon sexual attraction. He has no place in his life for love or marriage, and his predominant concern in the novel is in seeking a way of life that does not encumber him with the traditional obligations of middle-class existence. He is a self-centered free spirit, at once cynical and highly aware. He asks little of himself and expects even less from others. His strongest emotional tie in the novel is to Charles, with whom he shares a bond of strong, affectionate love.

If Sam represents a contemporary type, perfectly in tune with the bland, self-centered values of the 1970s, Charles is the dreamy romantic, slightly out of step with his times but yet very much a product of them. Charles is immersed in the world of rock 'n roll. Everywhere he goes, he is aware of songs on the radio, stereo, or juke box and relates the messages in the songs to his own life. His sense of reality is tied up with Bob Dylan's songs, or Janis Joplin's overdose, or Mick Jagger's search for satisfaction. Charles lives what appears to be an adult life, having his own apartment, working at a government job, searching for someone to love and for a lasting relationship, but his consciousness (and thus his true identity) is wrapped up in a more adolescent sense of life and love. He fixates upon songs because he identifies them with his more carefree youth in which he had fewer worries and in which he never felt sorry for himself. Now that he has fallen in love with Laura, he pities himself all the time, and his sister tells him that he is a juvenile, sometimes even infantile, egomaniac. "You deliberately make yourself suffer all the time," she says, "because then you can be aware of *yourself*" (82). Susan tells Charles that he allows Laura to dominate his consciousness because he has little identity of his own and even less sense of direction for his life. Being wrapped up in thoughts of Laura gives Charles a ready and seemingly noble excuse to avoid examining his own life. Susan believes that, because self-definition (or making something of himself) is too difficult for Charles, he prefers to invest himself in an emotionally dependent relationship with Laura that mimics a home, mother, and family life—all the qualities of security that a child would seek.

There seems to be much merit to Susan's claim that Charles is "infantile" (82) in his desires. Charles himself admits to having a childlike desire to escape reality by spending his days imagining scenes about Laura that never took place. He chides himself for being overly dependent upon food, an oral fixation that in Freudian terms signifies an immature sense of seeking emotional gratification. He keeps a number of Laura's cookbooks on hand as comforting symbols of security, and he dreams throughout the novel of a special dessert Laura used to make for him of cognac and fresh oranges. "He often craves that dessert, and the recipe is probably in one of those books, but he can't bring himself to look. He wants to think of it as magic" (16). Rather than make the dessert himself and end his craving (in essence, meet his own emotional needs), he prefers to hunger and long (both physically and emotionally) for an imaginary ideal that he hopes will appear one day by magic. Like a child, he prefers magical, wishful thinking to purposeful choice, and the metaphor of his childlike longing for the dessert is an apt symbol of his immature longing for Laura as the "magic" that will set his life right.

As Charles's personal life collapses around him, Laura increasingly becomes the ideal that holds his existence together. Clara's neuroses intensify into periodic disassociations from reality, while Pete becomes more and more emotionally demanding of Charles's time and attention. Sam loses his job and moves in with Charles, becoming an economic (and, at times, an emotional) drain. Pamela Smith, Charles's ex-lover, who has become a compendium of 1970s cultural clichés as a bisexual, feminist vegetarian, returns to plague Charles with her own emotional insecurities and problems that need resolving. Susan has fallen in love with Mark, a somewhat pompous and obtuse medical student who drives a maroon Cadillac, will not pollute his body with toxins, and is, in Charles's opinion, a "dress for success" phony who exemplifies the worst superficialities and shortcomings of youthful ambition.

In the midst of his loneliness and isolation, Charles further exacerbates his emotional dilemmas by asking Betty, a co-worker, out for a date. Charles is drawn to Betty because she is Laura's close friend, and he hopes to feel a certain closeness to Laura through Betty. It is from Betty that Charles learns that Laura has left her husband and is living in an apartment. Charles's immediate reactions are shock, delight, and hurt that Laura would leave her husband and not tell him. He gets Laura's phone number from Betty and anguishes over what to say when he calls her. He is worried that her failure to call him is a sign that she does not love him. He broods about his situation, much to the dismay of Sam, who believes that Charles's affection for Laura is "disproportionate" (242). Finally, he calls Laura.

She says she did not call because she needs time alone to figure out what she wants in life and does not want to be pressured by his emotional demands. Charles protests that he is not demanding, that he loves her and wants her back, and Laura responds, "I don't think you're thinking of me. I think you're thinking about what's best for you" (244). Charles replies that he loves Laura and asks to see her just one more time.

Driving to Laura's, Charles tries to understand "why he seemed so incapable of impressing upon her, why he had always—almost always—been incapable of impressing upon her, that he loved her and had to have her" (245). He enters Laura's apartment intent upon letting her know that he will not be dissuaded from his love for her.

"Stop thinking about yourself and think about me," Laura says. "I need peace. I don't need to be told what to do. I've lost Rebecca and my marriage has fallen apart and I can't find a job, and you're telling me it can be like it was before." "It can!" Charles asserts (256).

Laura wants Charles to leave, but he cannot bring himself to go. He wanders through the apartment instead, lost in reveries of Laura, and only agrees to go when she promises that he can return the next evening and she will make the special dessert of oranges and cognac.

Upon his return, in the novel's final scene and denouement, he brings Laura tulips in a ceramic pot and watches Laura as she peels the oranges and warms the cream. The dessert signifies the fulfillment of his deepest longings, a type of symbolic filling of his emotional hunger for Laura and the romantic ideal that she represents to him.

"I got my way," he says.
"You did," she says.
"A story with a happy ending," he says. (299)

A number of critics have commented upon the ending of *Chilly Scenes of Winter* as being too romantically facile and unrealistically happy, given the depth and range of complexities in the novel that have kept

Charles and Laura apart. To these objections, Beattie responds that "Charles has pursued this woman all through the book and he does get her. But you should understand by that point that he's a strange enough character and that they're mismatched enough that the rest of their life clearly isn't going to be easy. It's not as though it's just a frieze for all time that you can do with a movie camera and really capture something. The characters presumably still walk and breathe after the last period, and who knows what's going to happen?"[5]

Clearly, attempts to view the ending of *Chilly Scenes of Winter* as a happy union of two young lovers are greatly weakened by the novel's heavy emphasis upon romantic misperceptions of reality and the subsequent distortions in both understanding and feeling that such illusory notions bring to life. Charles himself states that "he has always had problems with reality encroaching on his fantasies" (140), and David M. Taylor sees Charles's idée fixe, his endless longing for Laura, as a romantic refuge, a form of emotional solace Charles seeks from the "psychic intrusions of relatives, friends, and acquaintances—each with his own nebulous yearning."[6]

In seeking to escape his drab and unfulfilling real life by positing a romantic ideal of perfect, blissful love, Charles is no different from one of his literary models and progenitors, Jay Gatsby, who psychologically and emotionally divorces himself from his mundane past to embrace the visionary and romantic ideal of his love for Daisy Buchanan. Certainly, comparisons of *Chilly Scenes of Winter* to *The Great Gatsby* are made more striking by the many references to *The Great Gatsby* in the novel. Charles is always after Sam to ride with him over to Laura's just so Charles can drive by the house and imagine that Laura is there. Sam never wants to go because he considers the whole idea "pointless."

"She might be outside," [Charles says].
"Just walking around at the end of the drive, soaking up the cold air?" [Sam responds].
"The light might be on."
"Of course the light will be on. She wouldn't be in bed this early."
"Then I want to see the light."
"What's this, *The Great Gatsby* or something?" (213)

When Charles insists that he is going to Laura's, Sam says, "Take me home. I can't bear to watch you make a fool of yourself" (214). Charles stubbornly persists, however, and proceeds to drive over to Laura's.

"I mean it," Sam says. "This is pathetic. It's not like you call her and write her and make yourself obnoxious. All you do is slink over there to look at the lights on in her house. If she killed somebody you'd take the rap for her, wouldn't you? The whole Gatsby trip."

"She wouldn't ever kill anybody."

"Yeah, but what if she was driving your roadster along and a woman ran out in front of it?"

"Okay, okay. Enough."

"What can I say that will talk you out of this dreary driving by her house?"

"Nothing."

"There's no point to it. What does driving by her house prove?"

"Nothing."

"You just intend to do it anyway."

"I just intend to do it anyway." (215)

Critics have seen parallels to *The Great Gatsby* in *Chilly Scenes of Winter,* comparing Charles to Gatsby, Laura to Daisy, and the slightly cynical, emotionally aloof, Sam to Nick Carroway. In response, Beattie states, "The spirit of what Fitzgerald was getting at was something I wanted to restate. I do see some similarities between the 1920's and 1960's—that whole idea of being in a frantic state and still seeing real-life possibilities. That was deliberate. So there are echoes there, but not that strongly. It's not a rehash of *Gatsby* by any means."[7]

The concept of romantic love and the inevitable distortions of perception and of self it engenders is certainly a major theme of *Chilly Scenes of Winter,* but, as Beattie states, it is not the novel's major focus, but, rather, an outgrowth of her concern to depict the milieu and consciousness of a period in American culture. Charles and his circle of friends are products of the 1960s, embodying the idealism and frenetic energy of a highly motivated, highly politicized generation that sought major societal reforms and vast personal growth. Entering into the 1970s, on the verge of turning thirty, and both needing and seeking a way to stabilize their lives, they find themselves isolated and lost, their efforts at self-definition largely purposeless and ineffectual. In typical romantic fashion, they look to their past and find no acceptable answers. "'The goddamn sixties,' Charles says. 'How'd we ever end up like this?'" (210).

After drinking with J. D., a friend and another lost soul, Sam says to Charles,

"Everybody's so pathetic. . . . What is it? Is it just the end of the sixties?"

"J. D. says it's the end of the world."

"It's not," Sam says. "But everything's such a mess." (187)

Like all romantics, they look to their past but find no helpful insights. "'I sure am waiting for that Dylan album,' Sam says. 'I really want to know what Bob Dylan's got to say in 1975'" (218).

Devoid of heroes, prophets, meaningful goals, Charles and his friends wander in a type of existential malaise, searching for a new faith, a new purpose—acting very much like their counterparts of "the lost generation" of the 1920s. They search for explanations of why their lives have come to such emotional standstills and wonder if their culture is to blame. In a Kentucky Fried Chicken restaurant, Charles "looks around at all the families eating fried chicken" and thinks, "America is getting so gauche. If there's a McDonald's in Paris, is the Colonel there, too? Kentucky Fried bones thrown around the Eiffel Tower?" (194). What metaphor, what value has their era given them to long for, and what image of American life do they see around them that would give their personal aspirations significance?

Charles's answer, of course, is undying, romantic love, but there is much in *Chilly Scenes of Winter* to indicate that even Charles suspects the illusions and self-deceptions, large and small, at the heart of his quest. He wants to live with Laura in a house that they have picked out together and bought, raise a family, and have a dog. Yet, he admits to himself that "it sounds too Norman Rockwellish to be true" (251). He knows that Clara and Pete's marriage did not last, that no one he can think of has a happy marriage, yet he still believes that he and Laura will be happy together forever. He bases this belief on the fact that they will communicate their problems to one another and work them out, but he also acknowledges that "they never really understood each other. Most people can read signals; they never could" (41). If Charles, by virtue of his romantic and idealistic longings in an age of jaded cynicism, is the moral center of *Chilly Scenes of Winter* just as Gatsby, the dreamer, was the axiological center of *The Great Gatsby,* he is, very definitely, a qualified and somewhat self-doubting romantic, and his quest for Laura's love is both strikingly noble and pathetic. This dual resonance of the dignity and foolishness of Charles's struggle to win Laura's love gives a greater dimension to *Chilly Scenes of Winter* than its surface context of the mores of the 1970s would seem to allow.

Critical Responses

In responding to *Chilly Scenes of Winter,* critics found much to admire in both Beattie's themes and her style. John Updike, in the *New Yorker,* stated that *Chilly Scenes of Winter* "thaws quite beautifully" with its "uncanny fidelity to the low-level heartbreaks behind the banal" and saw Beattie's work as comparable to that of Virginia Woolf and Nathalie Sarraute in achievement.[8] J. D. O'Hara, writing for the *New York Times Book Review*, commented that the novel was a "wide-screen panorama of Life in These United States" through which Beattie "understands and dramatizes our formlessness." Remarking that *Chilly Scenes of Winter* is "the funniest novel of unhappy yearning that one could imagine," O'Hara added that "Beattie renews for us the commonplaces of the lonesome lover and the life of quiet desperation. . . . The novel's major theme . . . is not waiting for an answer or Laura or love, but waiting itself, wistful anticipation, life unfulfilled and yearning. Immersing us in specificity, Beattie makes us feel these generalities on our pulse."[9] David Thorburn, in the *Yale Review*, praised Beattie's "powers of observation and dramatic representation" expressed in "a purified declarative prose not unlike good Hemingway" and judged *Chilly Scenes of Winter* to be a novel rich in "psychological nuance and in documentary power."[10] Thorburn's assessment was ratified by Sheila Weller who said of Beattie that "satirically, sadly, and truthfully, she writes of familiar fights against the damning arbitrariness of our charmed post-industrial lives."[11] John Romano emphasized the novel's sociological realism: "In *Chilly Scenes of Winter* . . . our attention is called to a contemporary pathos whose effects few have yet begun to gauge: the sadness over the passing of the 60's. . . . Beattie's presentation of Charles's nostalgia for the 60's suggests that such longing has the limits of an elegy to lost innocence, and the advantages, too. It distorts, but it also provides . . . the idea that things can be better than they are, because they have been better before now. As usual, the prospects for hope seem to depend upon some degree of mystification.[12]

In all, critics found in Beattie's depictions of hope and despair in the 1970s, through the "chilly scenes of winter" that represent the emotional seasons of the soul, a new voice and a strong, original talent. Praising Beattie's accomplishment in her first novel, critics applauded a significant writer on the contemporary scene and forecast even greater literary achievements from Beattie in the future.

Chapter Five
Secrets and Surprises
"Friends"

A focus upon the insufficiency of human relationships unites the stories of *Secrets and Surprises*. Characters test and cast off relationships as they would theoretical solutions, while marriages, love affairs, and friendships prove inadequate to meeting needs or sustaining the weight of ideal fantasies. Laurie Stone describes Beattie's characters as "the generation that turned friends into family, replaced family with friendship" and identifies the best stories in *Secrets and Surprises* as those that are about "the problems and paradoxes of heavily weighted friendships."[1]

The story in *Secrets and Surprises* that most clearly exemplifies Beattie's concept of the multiple roles friendship must assume in contemporary society is one entitled, appropriately enough, "Friends." The longest story in the collection, it depicts a group of friends, much like those in *Chilly Scenes of Winter*, who have known each other for years and have participated in and witnessed the full spectrum of personal changes the group has gone through.

The central character of the story is Perry, a somewhat passive and dreamy, highly romantic individual who watches his friends' emotionally complex and highly disordered lives while conducting his own secret love for Francie, an artist. Divorced from a husband who did not take her painting seriously, Francie lives by herself in a house in the New Hampshire woods. Perry romantically longs for Francie and contrives whatever means he can to be close to her and to share in her life. Francie, however, regards Perry only as a dear friend.

"A woman should have another woman for her best friend," Francie tells him, "but you're it." "Why would you have to have a woman for a best friend?" he asks her, and Francie responds, "It's hard for men and women to be best friends." Perry nods and Francie thinks that Perry has understood, "but all he meant to acknowledge was that they were close, but there was also something hard about that."[2] Though

pathos is associated with Perry's unrequited love for Francie, such longing is preferable to the emptiness of not being able to sustain the hope
that one day her friendship for Perry will develop into love.

As Perry endeavors to get closer to Francie and to find a right time
in which to suggest becoming her lover, their friends continually arrive
from various parts of the country, drawn by a desire to have parties at
Francie's or Perry's house and to spend time in the beauty of the New
England countryside. Perry bemoans the fact that his house "was a
wreck, after all, not because he didn't care enough to live decently, but
because his friends had taken it over and wrecked it" (244). Similar
upheaval and disruptions occur at Francie's as the friends use up her
house and leave their messes behind—an appropriate analogy for the
way in which they exhaust Francie and Perry emotionally, leaving their
problems and troubles for the two to resolve.

Freed, for example, has brought a young hitchhiker to the party.
The hitchhiker steals Freed's car and reappears later in the story to rob
Francie's house. Even the hitchhiker's complaints revolve around the
issue of friendship. He states that he stole Freed's car because the group
was not acting friendly towards him. "I was Freed's friend, but I'm not
good enough to be your friend, am I?" (255). Throughout the hitchhiker's diatribe and his threats, Perry is wondering "why some of their
friends who were always around didn't show up" (255). The hitchhiker
slashes one of Francie's paintings and steals her car; Perry feels ineffectual because he is unable to be brave and strong enough to wrest the
knife from the hitchhiker and end the terrifying situation before harm
is done.

Perry's ineffectuality with the hitchhiker matches his sense of frustration and despair in dealing with his feelings for Francie. Beth Ann
tells Perry that "everybody knows how you feel about Francie except
Francie. Or maybe she pretends not to know. I don't know" (231).
Perry feels sorry for Francie and "sorry for himself that he wasn't what
she wanted" (251). He nurtures the fantasy of finishing his house in
Vermont and asking Francie to come live with him. When he asks
Francie, he senses that she does not want to live with him. "I just don't
think of us that way," Francie says (247).

Perry's love for Francie is developed in the story in contrast to a
number of other relationships ostensibly based upon passion and love.
Some of the friends have formerly been lovers. Perry and Beth Ann
were lovers and lived together a number of years before, but their relationship has become highly distanced and perfunctory. Freed and De-

lores, however, have not let go of nor resolved the passion they shared ten years before. Delores lives with Carl; their daughter, Meagan, is the communal child for the group. At Francie's party, Delores and Freed rekindle their attraction. Carl leaves in a pique of jealous rage, and soon thereafter Freed and Delores run off together, leaving Meagan in Francie's care. Eventually, Freed and Delores leave Meagan with her grandparents so that they can "try to have a life" (249). Distressed at the couple's irresponsibility, Francie thinks of the immaturity and self-centeredness of her circle of friends, but realizes that she has no other friends. "I know a few other people," she says, "but I don't care anything about them. Sometimes when all of us are together we have good times. I don't want to make them all go away" (246).

In the story's denouement, Francie comes to live with Perry, although the motivations for her actions remain unclear. It is possible that she has chosen to be with Perry because she realizes how deeply she hurt his feelings in telling him that she did not think of him as a lover. It is possible, too, that she joins Perry out of loneliness and the feeling that any type of emotional bonding is preferable to isolation and withdrawal. Francie has become successful as a painter, and perhaps she wishes to share her success with someone, to have the emotional security that a successful career and a stable home life can create. In the midst of her friends' emotionally chaotic or emotionally sterile lives, she lives in a type of protected tranquility with Perry, who dotes upon her and is awed by her success.

Despite the fact that Francie has come to live with Perry, he still nourishes one unfulfilled desire. He wants to marry her and live happily together forever—although Francie has only "withering things to say about marriage since her own marriage had gone bad" and finds the exaggerated closeness of Nick and Anita, the one married couple in the story, "a little ridiculous" (261). As Francie prepares to be interviewed by a writer from the *Village Voice,* Perry watches the man arrive and pull up into the driveway. T. W. and his band are in the house, practicing; a puppy runs up to the interviewer and jumps around him in circles. Perry is amused to wonder if the man thinks he will be interviewing someone who lives in a commune. As Perry turns away from the window to answer the door, the phone rings.

Laurie Stone has described "Friends" as "profoundly disturbing": "All the characters are confused and inarticulate. 'I don't know how to talk,' Francie complains. 'I'm either alone and it's silent here all day, or my friends are around, and I really don't talk to them.' Most lead alarmingly chaotic lives, dangerous and endangered, fragmented and scattered. Having thrown out the old rules that made people feel stable, they are not strong or creative enough to invent replacements. Even more disturbing: The relationships described are the most important ones the characters have, yet it could easily be argued that no one is truly a friend to anyone else."[3]

"Friends" concludes, too, on what might be viewed as an ominous note. Throughout the story, the ringing of the telephone has brought only bad news or disruptions. Friends call in need of emotional support or with problems to be resolved; those without a problem need money or a place to stay. Perry's romantic dream of living with Francie happily forever, much like a fairy tale ending, has already been disrupted by the presence of T. W. and his band. Thus, friends, in the story, become an ambiguous or dualistic symbol; they provide comfort and support by their presence, but they also impede the type of intimate closeness that deeper relationships, like love affairs or marriages, require. As Stone suggests:

> Beattie's characters have placed great emphasis on friendship, but they haven't come any closer to understanding their relationships, or to finding intimacy and support in them, than their parents did in marriage. Beattie's characters crave connection, but have no idea how to achieve it, and while their dependence on friendship has increased, so has their disappointment. . . . The old facts of human relationships still apply for those characters; there are takers and givers, destroyers and restorers, bad people and good people, but it is unclear—Beattie's stories illuminate with splendid clarity—what any of this has to do with relatedness. It is unclear whether the dream of an extended family composed of free and floating individuals can ever provide what Beattie's characters want. It is also unclear whether any other arrangement of people can supply very much more.[4]

"Octascope"

A similar search for bonding and for a type of extended family to provide security in a complex and threatening universe is presented in the story "Octascope." The narrator is a young woman with a baby. She has been abandoned by a musician, who seems to be the baby's father. She is befriended by Nick, a man she met while waitressing, and is taken to live with Nick's friend Carlos, a marionette-maker. Though she prefers Nick to Carlos, she is grateful to have a place of shelter for herself and the baby. Carlos is described as "a kind person who wanted a woman to live with him" (103). The narrator says she went to live with Carlos "feeling like a prostitute" (103), but it is weeks before he touches her.

Carlos lives isolated from society and puts his energies into creating marionettes of cherrywood, peach, and birch with "slits and circles of eyes" that "glow at night like the eyes of nightmare demons" (102). Though the image of his marionettes suggests evil or the macabre, Carlos is a very gentle person, "a man totally dedicated to sensitive, craftsmanly execution of fantasy."[5]

The young woman spends much of her time trying to get Carlos to talk to her. She makes up lists of questions and reads them out loud to Carlos, hoping that he will respond. She also types up a list of facts about Carlos, some real and some imaginary, that she tries to elaborate out into a story of his life; she wants him to fill in the details and make himself more known to her, but Carlos remains quiet and aloof. When it is obvious by her reaction that he must say something, he asks if he should raise chickens or if they should continue to get eggs from his friend, Dime.

The tranquility of Carlos's withdrawal from society is interrupted when his friend Kirk takes a consignment of marionettes to New York to sell. The police stop Kirk's van, heavily decorated with antiestablishment bumper stickers, and suspect that he is running drugs. They open up the cardboard box that contains the marionettes and smile to themselves as they unwrap the packages of white towels. Finding only a bear wearing a vest, they smash the marionette in half with an axe to see if drugs are hidden inside. The incident confirms Carlos in his belief that "there is nowhere in the United States safe to bring up a baby" (105).

John Gerlach, in an interesting analysis of "Octascope," views the story as a study of passivity and withdrawal versus the contrasting attitudes of engagement and action. To Gerlach, "Octascope" is typical of a number of Beattie's stories in which a female protagonist "is generally not so much independent in her own right as forced to take action because of the stagnation, inwardness, and metaphorical or literal homosexuality of the males." However talented Carlos may be in making his marionettes, Gerlach contends, he is "still a man who in effect is playing with dolls." "The narrator at first seems much like Carlos, in every sense along for the ride and easily satisfied with imaginative solutions to all problems: when she finds there is no phone at Nick's house she holds her hand over her heart and sends telepathic messages to her aunt (with whom she had been living) to tell her that she was all right." But, as Gerlach points out, "the narrator has a sense of reflectiveness, inquisitiveness that is absent in the men."[6] When she rides in Nick's car to Carlos's house, she cannot resist catching glimpses of herself in the mirrors that are glued in several spots in Nick's car. She has a passion to know about Carlos and looks for clues in the medicine cabinet. By the end of the story, she wants to know where she stands with Carlos: "I have to know if we are to stay always or for a long time, or a short time" (108). While Nick and Carlos are gone, she steps outside and holds an octascope—a present from Nick to the baby—up to the scenery and feels "as powerful raising it to my eye as a captain with his periscope" (108). Gerlach points out that "if the men have abdicated action in favor of passivity, the narrator can be at least symbolically active. She has a passion to know, to explain, and to move that will probably leave her dissatisfied with Carlos."[7]

While Gerlach presents an intriguing view of "Octascope," locating the center of the story in the contrast between Carlos's passivity and the narrator's active desire to understand and to know, it is far more profitable, as well as far more consistent with the rest of Beattie's writings, to envision "Octascope" as a study of the limitations of human relationships. The narrator in the story is a displaced young woman, cut off from family connections. She has been abandoned by the father of her child and has been asked to move out from her aunt's home because the aunt is going to get married. She meets Nick as a stranger in a restaurant and rides with him to a stranger's home to live because she has no place else to go. She is pleased to find that Carlos is kind, but also feels like a prostitute in living with him under the terms Nick and Carlos have defined. Establishing a very pleasant homelife with Carlos, who provides for her economically and also helps with caring for the baby, the woman finds that she is much more attracted to Nick than she is to Carlos. Nick, though, is not interested in her nor in the domestic and emotional responsibilities she and the baby represent. Instead, he would rather go to the bars and be free to pursue more casual sexual involvements.

For the narrator to stay with Carlos or to go is not an easy choice. Her life with Carlos is pleasant, secure, and not especially demanding. But, if she stays, there is the possibility that she will become like Carlos himself—motionless and in retreat from the world. The complexity of her dilemma is magnified, both literally and symbolically, when she looks through the octascope. A child's toy, the octascope, might, one would suppose, make reality seem less complex and more congenial. As it is, the octascope, a kaleidoscope without the pieces of colored glass, makes the two animal marionettes hanging from the ceiling "proliferate into a circular zoo" (108). When the woman steps outside with the octascope, "in floods the picture: the fields, spread white with snow, the palest ripple of pink at the horizon—eight triangles of the same image, as still as a painted picture when my hand is steady on the Octascope" (108). "It will rain, or snow," the woman thinks to herself. "This is the dead of winter" (108).

Within the complex scene the octascope creates for the woman, change is imminent. Yet what, in "the dead of winter" is the decision to be? How is the woman to see reality—as complexly and diversely as the octascope reveals it to be, or as simply as she has previously viewed it by trusting other people and letting her life be shaped by their impress or suggestions? In Beattie's fictional universe, there are no clear-cut, simple answers, and certainly the insubstantial nature of human relationships provides no clues for unraveling or finding one's way out of the maze created by the octascope of vision and understanding.

"A Vintage Thunderbird"

In the various stories of *Secrets and Surprises,* it is often objects or animals that hold people together when love itself is insufficient to establish meaningful ties. In "Octascope," a fascination with the marionettes Carlos makes binds the woman to Carlos on a deeper level than does their interaction. In "Distant Music," two lovers befriend a scraggly puppy and stay together longer than they probably would have, had they not had the joint responsibility of caring for the animal. Stone comments that "if Beattie's stories are 'about' anything, it is the difficulty of locating" a "concept of meaningfulness in contemporary existence."[8] Those characters who cannot find this center of purpose in their present relationships often are forced to live on the muted spiritual energy of nostalgia or of idealized romantic fantasies.

"A Vintage Thunderbird" reveals Beattie's capacity for depicting characters immobilized by romantic longings. It focuses upon Nick and Karen, who were once in love. Nick remembers as the highlight of his emotional life the night Karen bought a white Thunderbird to celebrate her birthday. They had driven it through the Lincoln Tunnel, a streamer of orange crepe paper tied to the car's antenna. In New Jersey, he had driven, then she had driven, then he had driven again.

"Years later he had looked for the road they had been on that night, but he could never find it" (8).

When Karen begins to date other men, Nick finds that the hardest thing for him to accept is that "she did not mean to shut him out of her life" (4). Rather than lose Karen completely, he is willing to take the relationship on any terms.

> "Am I still going to see you?" Nick said.
> "I suppose," Karen said. "Although things have changed between us."
> "I've known you for seven years. You're my oldest friend." (7)

Embodied in Nick's plea for Karen not to discard their relationship completely but to value it for its length and depth is the poignancy of Nick's awareness that he loves Karen much more than she loves him. Thus, Nick is the powerless one in the relationship and Karen the powerful one. Unwilling to risk losing Karen's affection, even in the diminished and muted structure of a relationship rather than a love affair, Nick is essentially at Karen's mercy and must take the relationship on the terms she defines.

Nick is expected to be patient and understanding when Karen has an affair with a professor whom Nick regards as a pompous bore. Nick cannot understand Karen's interest in the man, and Karen is unwilling to explain herself to Nick. Karen expects Nick, however, to be available whenever she needs him for emotional support. The night Nick is dating Petra, Karen calls him at his apartment and tells him to throw out whoever is there and to come over to her apartment immediately. She needs to talk; Stephanie, her best friend, has decided at thirty-eight to have a baby, after much pressuring from her husband, Sammy. Karen thinks it is a terrible idea and needs Nick to comfort her through her anxieties.

Nick responds that he cannot come then but will come later. He takes Petra to a bar and rushes through his drink with her. He excuses himself to call Karen again, and then he tells Petra that he must leave. "Whoever the woman is you just called," Petra says, "I hope the two of you have a splendid evening" (9).

Nick leaves the bar to go to Karen's apartment and is mugged. His wallet is stolen and his wrist is broken. Too confused and embarrassed to see Karen, he returns to his apartment, hoping to build up the courage to call her. Instead, he receives a phone call from Stephanie. She has decided not to have the baby and has come to New York for an abortion. She is at La Guardia airport and wants Nick to pick her up.

Stephanie moves in with Nick while she tries to decide what to do about having the baby. Nick and Stephanie both try to reach Karen, but they are unsuccessful. Nick feels certain that Karen has gone off somewhere with the professor. Petra calls and arranges another date with Nick; then she stands him up. She calls to tell Nick that she is sorry and that she has never done that to anyone before. Nick says he would like another chance to take her out and make it up to her for the way he treated her the first time. Petra says she does not want to get involved with him. "I like you and it's a mistake, because I'm always letting myself in for it, agreeing to see men who treat me badly" (13).

Nick is aware that Stephanie, who has just entered the apartment, has overheard his conversation with Petra. In a fit of frustration, he rips the phone out of the wall. The gesture is not very successful; the phone line pops out of the jack, and Nick is left there ineffectually holding the phone in his good hand, his other hand still encased in a cast. "Would you think it was awful if I offered to go to bed with you?" Stephanie asks. "No," Nick says. "I think it would be very nice" (13).

Several days later, Karen returns. She has been to Bermuda with the professor. Nick wants to borrow Karen's Thunderbird and go for a ride to be by himself for awhile. "Her key ring was on the table. If he had the keys, he could be heading for the Lincoln Tunnel. Years ago they would be walking to the car hand in hand, in love. It would be her birthday. The car's odometer would have five miles on it" (14). Instead, he tells Karen of Stephanie's problem and of how Stephanie needs to see Karen. Karen questions why Stephanie has come to New York, and Nick replies, "Because we're her friends." "But she has lots of friends," Karen says (15).

Nick is shocked to realize that Karen does not understand that Stephanie has come to New York to see her, not him. "He had seen for a long time that it didn't matter to her how much she meant to him, but he had never realized that she didn't know how much she meant to Stephanie. She didn't understand people. When he found out she had another man, he should have dropped out of her life. She didn't deserve her good looks and her fine car and all her money" (15–16).

Later that day, Stephanie has her abortion. Nick calls Sammy, her husband, from a phone booth to let him know that Stephanie is all

right, and Sammy tells him that he could name Nick as corespondent
in the divorce case, since Stephanie called about the details of her involvement with Nick. "You know what happened to you?" Sammy
says. "You got eaten up by New York" (17). Sammy tells Nick that
Stephanie and Nick need to know that "you can be happy." Stephanie
could have chosen to have the baby and be happy, and Nick could
choose to get out of New York and forget Karen. "Do you know that
your normal expression shows pain?" Sammy says to Nick. "Do you
know how much Scotch you drank the weekend you visited?" (17)

Nick listens to Sammy's conversation and then returns to his apartment. Stephanie and Karen are both there. Karen had slept in the
apartment the night before, and the three of them had gone to the
abortion clinic at eight in the morning for Stephanie's abortion. When
Nick looks at Karen, he wants to tell her that "they should go and get
the Thunderbird, and as the night cooled, drive out of the city, smell
honeysuckle in the fields, feel the wind blowing" (20). But the Thunderbird has been sold. Karen told Nick the news while they were in
the waiting room of the abortion clinic. The Thunderbird had needed
a valve job, and a man she met in Bermuda—who coincidentally wanted to buy the car—told her to sell it. Even as Karen is telling him the
story, Nick is aware that she has been set up. "She had been conned,
and he was more angry that he could tell her. She had no conception—
she had somehow never understood—that Thunderbirds of that year,
in good condition, would someday be worth a fortune" (20). Nick's
feelings of hurt and anger at Karen's betrayal are so strong that "he had
had an impulse to get up and hit her" (20).

"When are you going to stop making such a big thing over it?" Karen said.
"That creep cheated you. He talked you into selling it when nothing was
wrong with it."
"Stop it," she said. "How come your judgments are always right and my
judgments are always wrong?"
"I don't want to fight," he said. "I'm sorry I said anything."

Karen puts her head on Nick's shoulder. "I just want to ask one thing,"
he says, "and then I'll never mention it again. Are you sure the deal is
final?" (20).

Karen pushes Nick's hand off her shoulder and walks away. She sits
on the sofa and picks up the newspaper; soon, she puts it down and
stares across the room into the bedroom where Stephanie is resting.

Nick looks at Karen "sadly for a long time, until she looked up at him
with tears in her eyes." "Do you think maybe we could get it back if
I offered him more than he paid me for it?" she says. "You probably
don't think that's a sensible suggestion, but at least that way we could
get it back" (21).

"A Vintage Thunderbird" is a thematically rich story, especially
when viewed in terms of Beattie's concept of the tenuous and often
perilous nature of human relationships in contemporary society. Perhaps the key to the story is the idea of understanding. Karen is lovely,
desirable, rich, and privileged, yet she has relatively little self-under-
standing or sensitivity to others. Nick possesses much sensitivity to
others but is immobilized by his romantic longings and his penchant
for living nostalgically in the past rather than facing some hard realities
about Karen and his own aimless life. Focusing upon memories and
recalling those memories only in the most ethereal and idealized terms,
Nick has essentially isolated himself from time and from the require-
ments of personal growth and maturity. The vintage Thunderbird is
the symbol of his romantic and youthful aspirations and dreams. With
the Thunderbird gone, Nick confronts the loss of his innocence and
the shattering of his illusions. He must see Karen in a new light, and,
perhaps saddest of all, he must deal with the painful realization that
Karen, as the object of his intense, romantic idealization, is not worthy
of his devotion and love.

The poignancy of Nick's disillusionment is heightened by the contrasting realistic elements in the story. Nick's treatment of Petra is
insensitive and self-serving, and Petra is compelled to admit to Nick
that she is always letting herself in for it by agreeing to see men who
treat her badly. Nick, Karen, Stephanie, and Sammy consider themselves close friends, but Karen largely wishes to pass Stephanie's problems off onto others, and Nick becomes involved in an adulterous
liaison with Stephanie that hurts Sammy deeply. The truest voice of
reason and insight in the story is, in fact, Sammy, who tells Nick that
people can be happy because they can let go of what causes them pain
and they can choose to content themselves with what they have. Sammy's insight registers with Nick, but he is unable to act upon it because he prefers to delude himself with fantasies about trips in the
Thunderbird with Karen and the belief that those days will somehow
come again. Unwilling to let go of the past and unable to content
himself with just being Karen's friend, Nick is lost in an entanglement
of conflicting and self-defeating emotions. He is forced into a moment

of enlightenment when Karen, insensitive to how much the Thunder-bird symbolizes to Nick, sells it to a person who values the car only for its monetary value. The loss of the Thunderbird, despite the anger and pain it causes Nick, appears ultimately to be a freeing act, engendering in Nick the realization that the past is truly gone and cannot, in Gatsby-like fashion, be recaptured and relived. Only with this realization is Nick free to act upon the concept of self-definition that Sammy has posited for him and to free himself of Karen's hold upon his life, just as Karen has freed herself from the sentimental and emotional bondage of the vintage Thunderbird.

"Colorado"

Were Ann Beattie a less philosophically complex writer, she would structure her fictional universe so that the fulfillment of romantic longings would provide happiness and contentment for her characters. As it is, Beattie is too realistic an author to hold that any experience or any human construct brings lasting happiness. The contemporary world is an ambiguous one, in which, as fiction writer Lee K. Abbott remarks, "the heart never fits its wanting," [9] and Beattie, as a neo-realist, is a faithful depicter of the inability of the human heart to find fulfillment in what it seeks.

Sheila Weller has described Beattie's characters as "the new lost generation," noting that, in their "secrets and surprises," they constitute a new generation of seekers who are metaphorically, and sometimes quite literally, lost within the complexities and conflicting philosophical demands of contemporary existence. [10] Characters like Nick in "A Vintage Thunderbird" or Perry in "Friends" sustain unfulfilled longings and predicate their lives upon nostalgic and idealized dreams of romantic love. Other characters, like Robert in "Colorado," attain their secret longings and find, to their surprise, that even idealized love is not enough to sustain them or to assuage feelings of aimlessness and despair.

Watching Penelope go through a series of emotionally vacuous love affairs, all the while wishing that she might someday be his, Robert enacts the pathos of unrequited love so central to many of the stories in *Secrets and Surprises*. When Penelope, on the rebound from an unhappy affair, asks Robert to run away with her to Colorado, he goes with her largely out of a sense of not knowing what else to do with his life. A would-be painter who is a Yale graduate school dropout, Robert hates New Haven and feels disoriented in conducting a life not committed to school, career, or a lasting love affair. Yet, when Penelope suggests an escape to Colorado, he feels equally confused about the value of leaving New Haven and breaking ties with his past.

"I know it's going to be great in Colorado," Penelope says. "This is the first time in years I've been sure something is going to work out. It's the first time I've been sure that doing something was worth it."
"But why Colorado?" he says.
"We can go skiing. Or we could just ride the lift all day, look down on all that beautiful snow." (145)

The image is a romantic one, of life removed from time, consequences, and care; it is exactly the idealized picture that someone like Penelope, who drifts from involvement to involvement and has no emotional stability or direction in her life, would seek. Beattie skillfully captures this concept in her description of Penelope as a member of "the new lost generation"; "she had flunked out of Bard and dropped out of Antioch and the University of Connecticut, and now she knew that all colleges were the same—there was no point in trying one after another. She had traded her Ford for a Toyota, and Toyotas were no better than Fords" (132).

When Robert and Penelope go to Colorado, they stay with Penelope's friends, Bea and Matthew, who are in the process of divorcing. Robert wanders in the woods and tries to paint rustic scenes; mostly, he gets stoned and contemplates the loss of direction in his life. Heavily stoned and driving to a liquor store with Matthew, Robert asks him, "What state is this?" "Are you kidding?" Matthew says, shaking his head. "Colorado" (154).

There is no meaningful resolution to Robert's quest for love and direction in his life. He wins Penelope's love, but it is a Pyrrhic victory. Dan, Penelope's former lover, told Robert the day before he left for Colorado that Penelope would kill Robert. "She'll wear you down, she'll wear you out, she'll kill you," Dan says (152). Lost in a haze of dope, Robert is as dazed and unaware of where he is and where his life is going, as he is in loving Penelope. The center of his life has been Penelope, and now the center will not hold. Colorado is New Haven, just as Penelope discovered that all colleges were the same and "Toyotas were no better than Fords." Romantic fantasies do not provide purpose in life, and, without a purpose in life and a committed sense of self-definition, Robert has become a type of existential drifter. Like "the new lost generation," he will always be asking "What state is this?" and always seeking ways to invest his life with meaning.

"The Lawn Party"

If "Colorado" takes a plaintive look at the dilemma that reality does not measure up to one's fantasies and thus all dreamers and questers are forced to live with disillusionment and despair, "The Lawn Party" presents Beattie's most vitriolic comment upon the futility of questing itself.

The lawn party takes place outside the window of an unnamed narrator. It is the Fourth of July, a day the narrator's father loves "better than his own birthday" (191). Most of the people at the party are wearing "little American flags pinned somewhere on their shirts or blouses or hanging from their ears" (191). Lorna, the narrator's ten-year-old daughter, has come to ask her father to join the party—a request that might be "dismissed with a wave of the hand, but I have none. No right arm, either. I have a left hand and a left arm, but I have stopped valuing them. It's the right one I want. In the hospital, I rejected suggestions of a plastic arm or a claw. 'Well, then, what do you envision?' the doctor said. 'Air where my arm used to be,' I said. He gave a little 'Ah, so' bow of the head and left the room" (192).

The setting of the lawn party leads the reader to believe that the narrator is a Viet Nam veteran refusing to take part in the superficial displays of patriotism engaged in by the company at the party. The narrator, though, is not an injured veteran; he has lost his arm in an automobile accident while involved in an affair with his wife's sister Patricia. "My sister killed herself and tried to take you with her," his wife tells him when he awakens at the hospital. "You deserved this," she says, and walks out of the room (193).

Losing his arm, Patricia, the passionate love of his life, his marriage, and his career as an artist, the narrator is left with a troubled relationship with his daughter, who, at ten, is too old and worldly-wise for the fairy tales and stories he wants to tell her, and the misplaced hero worship of Banks, one of his former art students. Unable and unwilling to relate to his relatives, the narrator removes himself physically and emotionally from their presence. He stays up in his room and watches

them, as he watches the world, from a distance. Lorna cannot persuade
him to leave his room, nor can Danielle, his brother John's wife. Danielle comes to the narrator in increasingly drunken states, urging him
to come downstairs and join the party. Instead, the narrator takes Danielle's foot in his hand and kisses it across the toes. "Stop it," Danielle
says, laughing. "Someone will come in." "They won't," the narrator
says. "John isn't the only one tired of my insults" (196).

Banks comes to visit the narrator to borrow five dollars to buy some
liquor and to find out what the narrator thinks of his paintings. "All
night I pray until I fall asleep that I will become great. You must think
I'm crazy. What do you think of me?" he says. "You make me feel
old," the narrator responds (203).

The narrator tells Banks the story of his love for Patricia. "What I'm
saying is that all was well in the kingdom. Not exactly, because she
wasn't my wife, but she should have been" (204). When the narrator
asks Banks what he thinks, he responds, "Banks's lesson. Never look
back. Don't try to count your tail rings" (204).

Outside, at the lawn party, "they've found a station on the radio
that plays only songs from other years. Danielle begins a slow, drunken
dance." The narrator looks at her and imagines "her dress disappearing,
her shoes kicked off, beautiful Danielle dancing naked in the dusk.
The music turns to static, but Danielle is still dancing" (205).

The narrator, once in search of ideal love, finds part of his physical
being—and symbolically his emotional being, as well—destroyed in
the loss of his love for Patricia. He is now only "the wounded presence"
who "observes the festivities with disdain and reluctance from an upstairs bedroom window,"[11] interacting openly with no one and keeping
himself at bay emotionally from all who would seek to make contact.
The narrator projects a calloused and indifferent front to the world,
ignoring or insulting his relatives, relating poorly to his daughter, and
isolating himself in a hard, cynical attitude of self-deprecation and
sarcasm that only Banks, for a brief moment, can penetrate. Yet, in
the last scene of the story, the narrator is lost in a romantic vision,
watching Danielle and imagining her dancing naked and free in the
dusk. Even in his isolation and withdrawal from the world, the narrator has unfulfilled longings for the ideal. In contrast to Robert,
Nick, or Perry, however, he will search no longer but remain in his
refuge, ignoring Banks's advice not to look back because the narrator
is unable to look beyond the limits of his own emotional entrapment.

Nihilistic Environments

Karla M. Hammond views the most powerful aspect of *Secrets and Surprises* as Beattie's ability to depict "nihilistic environments" in which characters feel isolated or trapped, but yet, in which there is also a concurrent sense of desperation entailed in having to make choices. She cites "the familiar strain of pessimism" that runs its course in Beattie's narrations and is developed in a "crisp, blunt style (reminiscent of Hemingway)." The comparison is apt, for Beattie does concern herself with depicting her characters' "futile attempts to nourish and protect each other" and "the aimlessness of those who are incapable of seeing anything through." And, as Hammond points out, "there is little stay against the displacement of these characters' lives. As in Samuel Beckett's 'Waiting for Godot,' one finds the anticipation without any logical resolution. Beattie's people, too, are caught up in the absurd—the more terrifying here though because it's not a dream world but chilling reality."[12]

If *Chilly Scenes of Winter* and a number of stories in *Distortions* reveal romantic elements in Beattie's work, it is obvious that *Secrets and Surprises* casts a skeptical eye upon that tendency and reveals Beattie's bitterly perceptive ability to unmask the illusions by which her characters have structured their lives. Stone finds in *Secrets and Surprises* that "a potent skepticism suffuses all of Beattie's fiction" and points out that "over the years, Beattie's doubts have grown deeper, darker, and more moving, and so has her fiction."[13] The ironic title *Secrets and Surprises* "hints at romantic possibilities, but the secrets turn out to be painful to know and the surprises unwanted."[14]

Dean Flower calls Beattie's characters in *Secrets and Surprises* "narcissists who can't bear to look at themselves," and perhaps in revealing the distortions that underlie the secrets and surprises of contemporary existence, Beattie has become, as Flower suggests, "an unsparing moralist of her generation."[15]

Chapter Six

Falling in Place

The publication of *Falling in Place* in 1980 marked a departure in Ann Beattie's themes and a new assessment of her skill as a writer. The scope of Beattie's vision had expanded: the new setting was suburbia, and the characters ranged from children to the middle-aged. The focus upon self-absorbed youths in search of romantic dreams and self-definition had shifted to the portrayal of "a family coming undone."[1] Critics who had previously dismissed Beattie as a "Johnny-one-note" writer exploiting the mystique of the 1960s grudgingly admitted that Beattie might possess more talent and depth than they had previously believed, and critics who had admired Beattie in her previous three works of fiction compared her to Chekhov, Cheever, and Updike in her "exactingly honest"[2] depictions of middle-class lives in emotional turmoil. Richard Locke, writing in the *New York Times Book Review,* proclaimed that "nothing Ann Beattie has written could quite prepare us for her new novel. It's like going from gray television to full-color movies. . . . *Falling in Place* is certainly, *faute de mieux,* the most impressive American novel of the season and establishes Ann Beattie not merely as the object of a cult or as an 'interesting' young novelist, but as a prodigiously gifted and developing writer who has started to come of age."[3]

The structure of *Falling in Place* differs dramatically from *Chilly Scenes of Winter,* a tale presented largely through conventional and essentially chronological narration. *Falling in Place* shifts from "conventionally presented narrative into short italicized chapters apparently designed to represent forms of inner consciousness, yet never suggesting the protagonists are entirely in control."[4] The form is highly reminiscent of Hemingway, a writer to whom Beattie is often compared, especially his *In Our Time,* in which a series of conventional narratives is interspersed with and disrupted by a set of thematically related vignettes. The purpose of the vignettes in Hemingway's volume is to provide subjective commentary upon the objective facts of the narration. The reader, unable to mold the two realms into a unified and satisfying perspective, is left with a dualistic vision that reenforces Hemingway's sense of the world, in our time, as fractured and diminished. In a similar fashion, Beattie uses the vignettes in *Falling in Place* to indicate that the divisions and pathos of the contemporary era cannot be so easily reconciled as societal myths and rationality might suppose. The subjective longings and needs of the characters in *Falling in Place,* expressed dramatically and poignantly in the vignettes, do not match up with the objective facts of their lives, and the novel raises the further issue of whether contemporary life itself, with its diminished values and dehumanizing structures, can ever satisfy the longings of the human heart.

Domestic Sorrows

Campbell Geeslin has stated that Beattie possesses a knack for showing us our world through artifacts,[5] and certainly this aspect of Beattie's work is made abundantly clear in *Falling in Place*. "Inside the suburban American house, in the far interior, is the horror, the horror."[6] "The suburban American house" in *Falling in Place* belongs to John Knapp and his family—his wife, Louise; his overweight and desultory ten-year-old son, John Joel; his self-absorbed and hostile fifteen-year-old daughter, Mary; and his five-year-old son, Brandt. All should be well in the Knapp family, for its members represent the epitome of the American dream and of upper middle-class stability; yet, all is very wrong. As Richard Locke has remarked, the reality is one of "domestic sorrows."[7] No one in the family is able to connect emotionally or to communicate well with the other family members, and each exists in an affectless and self-contained universe. The family looks like a family, poses itself into the accepted configurations of family life in suburban America by going on picnics and summer outings—but the family is a family in name only.

John and Louise have long since fallen out of love, and John has a mistress, Nina, with whom he is deeply in love, but for whom he does not have the courage to leave his wife and family. Louise has only a type of muted hostility for John; she tolerates him to keep the family together, but her actions and words indicate that she operates out of many bitter and resentful feelings. From her husband, Louise receives only distance and polite tolerance; the response from her children is openly hostile. John Joel finds her an inconsequential bore, and Mary, in the peak of her adolescent rebellion, considers her mother a barrier and an imposition. Louise's strongest attachments in the novel are to her friend, Tiffy Adamson, a stylish antifeminist suburban housewife, and to the memory of Mr. Blue, Louise's German shepherd hit by a car the previous summer. Louise mourns for Mr. Blue and feels deeper emotion for him than she does for John or for her children, largely because the dog was devoted to her and reciprocated her emotions. Her family, on the other hand, refuses to respond to Louise's needs; thus, ironically and pathetically, the memory of the dog has a more powerful effect on Louise's life than the realities of her present existence.

The family's emotional disjunctions are represented by its physical disruptions. John lives with his mother in Rye, New York, during the week and travels to his Connecticut home on the weekends. Originally, he moved in with his mother when he thought she was dying of cancer. When that diagnosis proved incorrect, John stayed ostensibly because the commuting distance to his job in New York City was shorter from Rye than from his home in Connecticut. In truth, however, living in Rye gave him the emotional and physical distance from his family that he desired and also placed him closer to Nina. To help add purpose and meaning to his mother's life, John has brought his son Brandt to live in Rye. Louise is aware that Brandt is growing away from her emotionally, since she sees him only on weekends, but she accepts his distance as only one more rebuff from her children.

John Joel and Mary live in the separate worlds of their different age groups and particular interests. John is obsessed with eating. He spends most of his time in a large tree in the yard, high up on the tenth branch, looking down upon the family and its doings. When he does descend, it is in search of food. His best friend is Parker, an equally troubled youth with a rebellious attitude and an eating problem to rival John Joel's progression toward obesity. The two hang out together and often go into the city to see movies or to go to museums. Parker is a street-wise youth who is clever and devious and never hesitates to manipulate others to his advantage. He wheedles money from John Joel for food and takes advantage of his innocence to get John Joel to do what he wants. Parker smokes a pack of cigarettes a day, keeps a stack of pornographic magazines to whet his developing sexual interests, and is in prolonged psychotherapy with a child psychologist to help him change his negative responses and adjust to his environment. Parker is as hostile toward his family as the Knapp children are toward theirs. He repeatedly lies to his mother to get more money from her for food and magazines, and, as a symbol of his contempt for her, he has punctured a hole in her diaphragm with a pin.

It is interesting to note that all the children who play a significant role in *Falling in Place*—Parker, John Joel, and Mary—possess no true childhood innocence, imitate adult ways, and harbor deep feelings of hostility toward their parents. Joshua Gilder has commented upon "the unanimous immaturity of Beattie's adults and the adultomorphization of her children,"[8] while Pico Iyer, in "The World According to Beattie," states that

it is the dark and perverse paradox of this country's broken families that adults and children have effectively changed places. . . . While all too many adults still lust after adolescence, all too many kids are thrust into a precocious maturity. Forced to fend for themselves, to walk a tightrope between the sins of their fathers and the vices of their peers, more and more children are hustled by privilege and negligence into a hard wisdom they must reluctantly assume. . . . In Beattie's stories, children are knowing before they are discriminating. . . . Even as these children are turning into tough little realists, their parents are tumbling into stolen romances and irresponsible rites, belatedly courting an innocence they had earlier squandered. . . . It is sad that the children of Beattie's world are afraid, confused, disenchanted; it may be sadder that their elders are no wiser and no better off.[9]

Perhaps most emblematic of adolescent rebellion and "adultomorphization" in the novel is Mary. Largely because she is, at fifteen, in the midst of puberty and on the verge of adolescent self-sufficiency, and largely because she is most aware of the deceptions and insensitivities by which her parents have shaped their lives, Mary focuses many of the themes of *Falling in Place* in her deep and brooding cynicism.

Mary is most alive emotionally in her room, a typical teenage bedroom bedecked with posters and the appropriate paraphernalia of youth. She has an obsessive crush upon rock star Peter Frampton. With six identical posters of him in her room, she often presses her body against Frampton's picture and kisses his lips, hoping that he will someday return her kiss with equal passion and love. Mary's longing for Peter Frampton and her intense belief that she can, through the intensity of her desire, make Frampton respond to her love, would be comical were it not for the fact that Mary's desire to have someone to love is representative of much of the emotional pain that many of the characters go through in *Falling in Place*. Each longs for more fulfillment than he or she possesses, and each believes that intensity of desire alone can make love real.

This fracture between the ideal and the real, between what one imagines in life and what one receives, is represented in the novel very graphically by John's dual life and also by the dual life of Cynthia Forrest, Mary's summer school teacher. Working on a Ph.D. in literature at Yale and teaching high school English during the summer for economic survival, "Lost in the Forest," as her students call her, is psychologically brutalized by her students' attitudes of hostility, boredom, and indifference. Endeavoring to teach the great books of Western civilization to students impervious to formal learning and too imperceptive to get anything of value from their assignments, Cynthia wonders

how could the students not care about the pilgrimage to Canterbury? How could she care that such idiots did not care? . . . But where did sophistication get you? It got you selected for an education at a classy college, and when you graduated, this kind of part-time job was the best thing you could get, and the pay was no good, and your brain—after so much time realizing that she *had* a brain—was now being challenged by trivia. . . . By the time her education was completed, her brain would be worn down to a little stub, pencil shavings on the floor.[10]

Cynthia's emotional state is equivalent to that of many of the characters in the novel. Dreaming great dreams of sophistication and the life of the mind, she is nonetheless trapped by circumstances and forced to redefine her identity and her expectations in terms of not the ideal, but the real. Her cynicism is generated by frustrated romanticism and by a genuine inability to find anything in her existence to measure up to her needs or her dreams.

Cynthia lives with Peter Spangle, who is also Nina's ex-lover. Spangle is a characteristic Beattie creation, similar in many ways to the confused, yet charming, males who inhabit *Distortions* and *Secrets and Surprises*. Georgia A. Brown envisions Spangle as "the quintessential Beattie hero: predictably unpredictable, in and out of jobs, cities, countries, apartments, beds; romantic, eccentric, childish; wanderer, prankster, potential deliverer."[11]

Spangle lives off an inheritance that he squanders and seems to have no higher ambition in life than the pursuit of hedonistic pleasures.

While Cynthia is serious, ambitious, and highly motivated, Spangle is zany, apathetic, and skeptical of ambition and achievement.

At his mother's urging, Spangle goes to Madrid to bring back his brother Jonathan, so that Jonathan will abandon a life of sensual pleasure and enter law school. When Spangle is gone for a long time, Cynthia begins to fear for his safety. Spangle, however, has returned from Madrid and not told Cynthia. He is spending time with Nina and endeavoring to win back Nina's love. The two spend the night together, but not as lovers; the next morning, there is a knock on the door. John has come to tell Nina that John Joel has shot Mary.

The Dream of Salvation

John Joel's shooting of Mary has shattered John's life and revealed to him the emptiness of the charade he has been playing with his family in pretending that he is a loving father and that his is a loving family. John Joel's act of violence has removed the mask of pretense that has surrounded the Knapp family, and John is forced to envision his life from a realistic perspective devoid of self-deceptions and poses. What he sees distresses him greatly.

He had been on his way to his Connecticut home because Louise had called and asked him to come. John had assumed she was going to tell him that she wanted a divorce. He felt a certain kind of sadness in realizing that his marriage had deteriorated to this point, but, as he tells his friend Nick,

his sadness wasn't really much about what he was losing: Visiting rights would give him as much time with Mary and John Joel as he spent with them now; and if he gave Louise what she wanted and she was halfway reasonable, they might even be friends in the way they hadn't been friends for years. His sorrow was that he felt he was losing so little. Or maybe he had lost a lot, fast, years ago; he had lost it and the loss had never caught up with him, and now he didn't feel much emotion about saying that it was gone (212).

As he drives to his home in Connecticut, John is expecting a calm, if somewhat melancholy, discussion with Louise about the terms of the divorce; instead, when he arrives, he finds police cars in his driveway. He learns that John Joel was playing with a gun that Parker had given him, had taken aim at Mary, believing the gun was not loaded, and had shot her in the side. "She was a bitch," John Joel says when John goes into his hospital room, seeking explanations (257).

John Joel has been hospitalized for psychiatric supervision and care. John, looking at his son, realizes how distant and alienated from his family he is—more isolated than even his living in Rye and visiting on the weekends has revealed to him. As Cynthia's friend Bobby states, "Just a few seconds determine everything" (251), and in those few seconds John's life has taken on a clarity that it never possessed before John was forced to confront the emotions welling beneath the surface of his family life. As John says to Nina of his children, "When they were babies I never thought they'd be children, and when they were children I kept thinking of when they'd be grown. I didn't think that somewhere in the middle there'd be a gunshot" (276).

The gunshot marks the thematic and structural turning point of *Falling in Place*. Prior to the shooting, John had been tied to his family by bonds of guilt and responsibility. Nina, in fact, accuses him of being a coward in failing to face up to the truth and the implications of his feelings for her. John chastises himself even more strongly— envisioning himself as both a coward and a hypocrite in leaving his family but not totally cutting the ties, in allowing the joy he feels in loving Nina to be minimized or destroyed by his weekend journeys to his family in Connecticut. The bind he faces is epitomized by his love for Nina. "She was ten years older than his daughter. He could slam balls into a wall for a million years and it would never get rid of his frustration that he had married the wrong person and had the wrong children" (34). He wonders what he would do if he were granted just one wish. "He thought that the wish should be a selfish one, not a wish to change things for other people, but a wish for self-salvation, a wish that dared whatever force governed wishes to come through: that his family all disappear in a puff of smoke, and that he could start over again with Nina" (301). The psychiatrist tells John that he identifies with John Joel's act of violence and that John would like to vent the same feelings of hostility if given the chance. But John knows that the psychiatrist is wrong. "It wasn't John Joel he identified with, but Mary. He was the victim, not the one who pulled the trigger. He certainly did not think that he had charge of his own life" (302).

Louise had summoned John to the family home in Connecticut not to ask for a divorce but to ask John to take the family on a vacation to Nantucket. Sitting in Mary's hospital room, looking at his daughter who has just been shot by his son, John realizes the impossibility of continuing the pretense of family love and togetherness. "What would he do with them in Nantucket? Go to the beach. Sail. Watch clouds change shape. Buy fudge. Post cards. He couldn't. He could do it for a week, two weeks, but he couldn't do it for the rest of his life" (288). Facing the truth of his feelings, John calls Nina to tell her that he is leaving Louise and that he wants to marry Nina.

"Mary had told him to be where he wanted to be, and he was going to take her at her word. The psychiatrist was in the business of fixing people up, and he could fix John Joel. Louise did not love him. She was paranoid about things that were not happening and she didn't care about things that were. The night he had stood looking at the shooting star, she had said to him that she didn't know everything and she didn't want to know" (333). While Louise chooses the shelter of illusions and partial knowledge, John's act of existential self-definition is to be faithful to his feelings and to accept the consequences of his choices. Guilt is no longer an acceptable basis for a relationship, and duty is no longer an adequate substitute for love. In finally cutting his ties to his family, John frees himself for a more complete and fulfilling love with Nina. The image is a highly romantic one in that John identifies Nina with both youth and the capacity to start one's life over again, but the tempered romanticism of the ending of *Falling in Place* stands in a hopeful (even if poignant) contrast to the melancholy enervation that has characterized John's life and the life of the Knapp family prior to John's decision to leave. In freeing himself from his family, John, perhaps, also frees them, for their lives have been encased by lies and defined by misperceptions and distortions.

Groups and Generations

Robert Towers envisions *Falling in Place* as structured around characters who fall into groups that are accidentally linked, thus emphasizing the novel's thematic focus that events in human lives and human relationships just happen to fall into place and are not the result of conscious self-definition and control.[12] The most important group of characters in the novel is clustered around the Knapp family. The generation represented by John Knapp is approaching middle age while still maintaining youthful dreams of success and a meaningful existence. A Princeton graduate, John is an affluent advertising executive who has worked the American dream to his advantage but who has been unable to attain a satisfying emotional life. His wife, Louise, also participates in the trappings of upper middle-class success, but she defends herself from the emptiness of her marriage by becoming embittered and sarcastic. Both John and Louise are unable to communicate effectively with their children, and each seeks emotional sustenance outside the marriage. John has his fashionable and protected affair with Nina, and Louise, her equally fashionable friendship with Tiffy Adamson.

The second grouping is composed of unmarried people still in their twenties and includes Nina; Cynthia; Spangle; Spangle's friend Bobby, a hyperactive poet who tries to become romantically involved with Cynthia while Spangle is away in Madrid; and George, a half-crazy magician who meets Cynthia in a laundromat and makes her the object of his obsessive romantic quest.

Both constellations are composed of unfulfilled people who have difficulty communicating honestly and making emotional contact. Towers describes the characters in the novel as operating out of a philosophical and emotional position that reflects "a minimum of self-recognized affect or commitment."[13] The group approaching middle age, represented by John and Louise, has achieved the American dream and found it wanting; its members have forged marriages and begun families and have found both activities more numbing and oppressive than fulfilling and redeeming. The younger group of characters is highly skeptical of the values that the Knapp family represents, yet its members are unable to posit viable alternatives. They drift like Spangle, or work at jobs not equal to their education and training, like Cynthia and Nina. When direction cannot be found and self-mastery seems a purposeless ideal, drugs and casual sexual involvements offer sufficient temporary distraction from emotional emptiness and despair. Love relationships in the younger group are founded upon very little other than convenience. Spangle returns to Cynthia, in part, because he cannot have Nina, yet never resolves his original complaint "not that Cynthia has done anything wrong, but they were beginning to seem like an old married couple" (269). Cynthia acknowledges Spangle's self-centered and less than committed ways, but takes him back mainly because she feels that any relationship is better than the loneliness she experienced while Spangle was gone. "She had put in so many years with Spangle—a lot of them because he wanted it more than she ever had—so that by staying away, he was withholding more than himself from her. With him gone, part of her past was gone, and that was hard to deal with because the present wasn't any too happy" (246).

Ironically, John and Nina, the most important members in their respective groups, speak of salvation and the survival of romantic love essentially in terms of transporting one's affiliations from one group to the other. In fact, John Calvin Batchelor views *Falling in Place* as "an overlapping series of bittersweet short stories, organized loosely into two love triangles that intersect at the point called Nina."[14] Spangle is in love with Nina and seeks to reestablish a relationship with her because he believes in her capacity to redeem him through love. John and Nina share a similar vision about each other. Nina tells John of a dream she had when they first met in which she is bobbing in the water with Louise, John Joel, Mary, and Brandt. John is in a boat large enough to take only one of them on board. Sometimes John would reach for her, sometimes he would reach for one of the others. Whenever he did reach for someone, everything in the dream became blurry, and then Nina was somewhere looking down, "puzzled because what was in the boat was a starfish, or a sea nettle, a sea anemone, a water lily, a conch shell. Some small, beautiful sea creature would be in the boat with him." After Nina told John the dream, she was embarrassed because the dream indicated that she thought he could save her. John made light of the dream. "The truth was that he did not think of her as someone who needed saving. He thought that she could save *him*, that her light grip on his arm, as they sat on the top of the dune, was anchoring his body to the earth." John feels that he never knows what to say when Nina is so honest. "He didn't know how to say, simply, okay, if you think that having me will save you, you can have me. If he could really have believed that he would be leaving Louise and the children to save *her*, then he probably would have done it instantly, but he was sure that he was leaving to save himself" (214–15).

Batchelor argues that John and Nina are trying to experience a type of symbiotic passage to adulthood. Nina is attracted to John because she is bored with her life and seeks the kind of paternalism John has to offer so that she can remain a "childish doper," and John longs to recapture his youth through Nina so that he, too, can reestablish both his innocence and his adult selfhood.[15] The irony, of course, of their pursuits and visions is that each has romanticized the identity and the stage in life that the other possesses. John's adult life is emotionally sterile, and all his affluence, which Nina so greatly admires, has not brought him happiness. Nina's youthful innocence glowingly covers a lack of direction and motivation. To exchange one phase and one set of group affiliations for the other seems not only a Pyrrhic victory but a confusion of idealism with self-deceit.

Perhaps the finest touch of irony in *Falling in Place* is represented by George, the magician, who falls in love with Cynthia and literally showers the path to her doorway with rose petals. George is as obsessively in love with Cynthia as John is with Nina, or Cynthia is with Spangle. He hides by Cynthia's apartment building and waits to catch glimpses of her. He met her in a laundromat and performed magic tricks for her by making pink sponge rabbits appear and proliferate; afterward, outside Cynthia's door virtually day and night, he dreams of making his love for Cynthia as dramatic and visible as the pink sponge rabbits. When Cynthia leaves her apartment one afternoon, the magician points a red water pistol at Cynthia and shoots her with a plastic rose. In his quest to win Cynthia's love, he is unfailing and totally dedicated. His devotion to Cynthia is the epitome of romantic love, and yet the magician's very actions and the intensity of his pursuit are comical and absurd.

As the comic relief in the novel to the sadness and poignancy of the interpersonal relationships "falling in place" in both Connecticut and New York, the magician's saga points out, by contrast, the absurdity that underlies all quests for lasting, romantic love. The quests are as illusory as the pink sponge rabbits the magician makes appear; yet, for the period that they distract and entertain, they provide a type of framework for existence, balancing that which is sought in its highest ideal with that which is attained in its formulated reality. As the magician states, "It's a rotten world. No wonder people want answers. No wonder they want to have parties and get distracted" (341). The magician also contends that "people love to think that things can be easy" (340). Things can, indeed, be easy, if they "fall in place," but there is little in the novel to indicate that ease, passivity, and "falling in place" (a type of metaphorical analogy to the Woodstock generation's aphorism of "going with the flow") are in any way identical to personal happiness.

Wasted Lives and Undying Love

Critics have contended that the structure of *Falling in Place* is too noncohesive to qualify the work as a novel. Both Batchelor and Towers maintain that *Falling in Place* is best viewed as a series of short stories rather than as a novel progressing through the conventions of character and plot development.[16] Tied to their objections is a belief that looseness of plot structure is equivalent to or a manifestation of facile artistic vision. Indeed, *Falling in Place* has been criticized as soundly for its amorphous structure as it has for an ending that seems too happy for the plot and characters of the novel. Clearly, however, to regard the fact that John and Nina, and Spangle and Cynthia, get back together at the novel's end as evidence of a happy, romantic ending is to miss much of the novel's focus upon the deficiencies of human relationships in contemporary society. There is much in the novel to indicate that Cynthia and Spangle are drawn to each other and stay together because they expect so little of each other. Their relationship has the ease and familiarity of the known, and little else. No strong emotional or passionate love unites the two; they have opted for letting their lives "fall into place," and clearly the type of relationship they make is indicative of the passivity and lack of self-definition that shape their lives.

John and Nina's union at the end of the novel is an even further indication of Beattie's ironic and skeptical intent. Each hopes the other will prove to be a savior, a rescuer of lost or wasted lives; each hopes to live vicariously through the other. Beattie has given enough evidence in the novel of the shallowness of these beliefs to indicate that John and Nina's relationship will be similarly founded upon self-deceptions and wishful thinking—not a very solid foundation for a relationship, to be sure. Further, Nina appears to be superficially attracted to John's wealth, just as John is drawn to Nina emotionally as a type of mother substitute.

In discussing his separation from Louise with Nina, John senses that Nina feels deeply responsible. "You talk as though you were a magnet," he says to her, "as though I had to be pulled along." Nina responds,

"I *was* a magnet. . . . I had advantages she didn't have. I *did* pull you along."
"What advantages?"
"Because I'm young, and she's not. Because I have this small quiet place for you to be, and at home it's the way you always tell me when you have a barbecue or something awful like that. You like it here because you're left alone."
"I could be in a cave and be left alone."
"It *is* a cave. . . . It's *cramped,* it's not cozy. I hate it that you love it so much, that you have so much and you want so little."
"What do I have? . . . Pillars at the end of my driveway. What else?

"Acres of land. Children. A big house. Try to *realize* what you have."
"You're what I want." (323–24)

In this exchange, there is an emphasis upon being dissatisfied with
what one has and wanting something else in its place, and there is a
concomitant irony to the fact that Nina would exchange her cramped
apartment for John's spacious house in the country, while John would
readily abandon his house to stay within the womblike confines of
Nina's apartment. The image is one of escapism rather than ideal love,
and it is difficult to maintain a critical perspective that interprets Beattie's uniting John and Nina at the end of *Falling in Place* as the typical
romantic ending of living happily ever after. If the discrepancies in
John and Nina's relationship are not sufficient to indicate the errors in
this view, consider John's statement after weathering his daughter's
shooting and after leaving Louise for Nina: "He wanted to think that
it was over, but actually very little of it was over. Nobody knew yet
what damage had really been done to all of them" (322–23). Clearly,
Beattie's perspective is not romantic or even facile, but deeply cynical.
Beattie focuses in *Falling in Place* on the damage done, and whether
love—especially the type of love that John and Nina share—can heal
all wounds and overcome all difficulties remains ambiguous.

The suggestion that the amorphous structure of *Falling in Place* vitiates the impact of the novel's thematic concerns seems effectively
countered by Jack Beatty's contention that "drift in a novel is not therefore what we have always thought it, an artistic weakness, but a profound comment on the way we live now. We drift, characters in the
novels that represent us drift, all God's former children drift." Comparing *Falling in Place* to Joseph Heller's *Something Happened* in its depiction of the American dream as a cheat, Beatty asserts that the
characters in *Falling in Place* are a "paradigmatic assemblage" of life in
the contemporary era.[17] If existence and relationships are disjointed and
complex today, why should contemporary artists like Ann Beattie be
forced to render such realities by means of conventional narrative patterns—linear plots, consistent character development, and the resolution of tensions via moralistic answers provided conveniently at the
novel's end? Why not the use of "assemblages" (or narrative collages)
to indicate that much in contemporary existence does just "fall in
place" and that characters who shape their lives in terms of that passive
acceptance of circumstances cannot be "developed" in the usual
fashion?

Certainly central to Beattie's concept of characterization in *Falling in Place* is a focus upon rendering characters primarily through dialogue rather than through an emphasis upon plot and action. In her review of *Falling in Place*, Georgia A. Brown maintains that what is most distinctive and interesting in Beattie's work is the voice, "the rendering in flat naive prose—simple declarative sentences, basic diction like primary colors, often a present tense that abjures reflection—of a contemporary near-pathologic sensibility." Brown argues that it is Beattie's literary sensibility, her sensitivity to the mores of her time, that is her most significant quality as a contemporary author. Further, the poignancy with which Beattie renders the contemporary scene points out the ennui, despair, and alienation of the last decades of the twentieth century. In Beattie's fictive universe, "admissible emotions are longing, melancholy, resignation, restlessness, wry or cynical amusement." Beattie's "toneless, dessicated prose renders as interior landscape this numb and inert universe. . . . The absence of strong feeling is a condition of being in this world; nothing erupts."[18]

"Being in this world" is equivalent thematically in the novel to "falling in place": "people don't shape their own destinies—they stumble upon them and then slide along forever."[19] As John Calvin Batchelor states, "recall that gravity is the most potent yet at the same time the most passive of forces."[20] Translate this sense of passivity into thematic and philosophical terms, and the vision of *Falling in Place* is defined. Brown calls the work a "relentlessly naturalistic novel," citing its capacity "to proceed digressively as cumulations of detail, information, and anecdote," while at the same time revealing the darker truths that reside within "the patently corrupt little world called family." Within the family, children dream, rebel, and enact violent impulses; rejection, confusion, and isolation seem their natural states. Adults, generally unwilling to act upon conscious choices, prefer magical thinking. "In the novel's world the emotion *longing* translates into the act *wishing*."[21] The novel, in fact, ends upon the idea of wishing. Spangle returns to Cynthia, telling her that he has lost the key to her apartment because his brother threw the key into a fountain in Madrid to make a wish upon. "What did he wish for?" Cynthia asks. "I don't know," Spangle responds. "The usual, I guess" (342).

It is an even further irony of Beattie's vision that even one's wishes are "the usual, I guess"—indistinguishable from the longings and dreams of others, largely because the contemporary world offers so little to capture and sustain the romantic imagination.

Gravity, Inertia, and Delay

Georgia A. Brown comments that "the generation Beattie writes about is popularly known for its addiction to instant gratification" and notes that interestingly, however, what Beattie writes are "narratives of postponement."[22] Clearly, the focus in *Falling in Place* is upon the concept of postponement—John and Nina postpone their relationship while John delays dealing with his unhappy marriage; Spangle puts off returning to Cynthia while he tries to renew his relationship with Nina; and Louise postpones trying to understand the problems in her marriage. Planting her garden, Louise reflects that "she had gone on sprinkling seeds, evenly, looking to see where they hit the dirt. They were so tiny that of course she couldn't see. She would see when they came up. She would find out what was going on with John when he left her" (97).

Not knowing is a type of comfort, a protected darkness, for illumination, with its concomitant disillusionment and anguish, waits as steadily to arise as the seeds Louise has planted wait to germinate.

Richard Locke has characterized Beattie's perspective in *Falling in Place* as a kind of "tepid nihilism."[23] Certainly, the novel does take a pessimistic view of most aspects of human endeavor, especially love and familial relationships, and very little in the novel is resolved neatly by the novel's end, "but rather in the vague, unsatisfying way things tend to be resolved in real life."[24] As a neorealist, Beattie has achieved her goal in *Falling in Place* of revealing the contemporary era in all its ambiguities and vacillations. "Settings, life styles, and values are dramatized with the precision of a period novel,"[25] and many of the insights Beattie reveals confirm the precarious nature of human interaction in the contemporary period. Beattie has stated that the major theme of her writings is the breakdown of communication and that "a direct result of this breakdown of communication is the breakdown of relationships."[26] *Falling in Place* represents Beattie's most extensive and intriguing investigation of the issues involved in the breakdown of relationships. The perspective she provides on why things "fall in place," "fall apart," and "fall in place" again is a focus upon, as Beattie states, "the artifices [that] assist in helping people delude themselves."[27] If self-knowledge illuminates, Beattie's characters in *Falling in Place* seem, paradoxically, especially comfortable and especially tormented in the dark.

Chapter Seven
The Burning House

In "The World According to Beattie" Pico Iyer has commented upon the irony of the title of *The Burning House,* Ann Beattie's third collection of short stories:

> Nothing seems to be "burning"; on the contrary, Beattie marked out the frosty and fragmented terrain that has become her own with the title of her first novel—*Chilly Scenes of Winter.* Her stories are archetypally set in winter, when snow eradicates color, contour, and contrast, when fingers and lives seem numb, when people, shuddering, can claim to be cool. Hers is not, to be sure, the anorexic pallor of Joan Didion's cardiograms of stunned or shattered nerves. Nor is it the overheated whiteness of Emily Dickinson, staring so intensely at a single spot that she grows dizzy. Beattie's is the white of hospital sheets and muffled December fields; not neurosis, but paralysis.[1]

Echoing Iyer, Daniel Zitin describes the stories in *The Burning House* as "bleak in both form and content. The bleakness is what marks them as Beattie's work, and doubtless it is their unity of theme and technique, the consistency and relentlessness of their sad vision that gives them their strong claim on our attention."[2] Affirming the significance of *The Burning House,* Dean Flower asserts that "these are stories of loss and emotional dearth, *Chilly Scenes of Winter,* about people so stuck in failing relationships that they're *Falling in Place.*"[3]

The "sad vision" Zitin notes in *The Burning House* is confirmed by the titles of several stories in the volume: "Learning to Fall," "Gravity," "Waiting," "Afloat," and "Like Glass." As Iyer notes, the stories are "preoccupied with weightlessness and drifting, with water and air. Characters do not sink or swim; they float, or—as the modish phrase has it—they go with the flow." Beattie "has always created metaphors that precisely reflect such off-balance lives slipping out of control."[4]

If events and relationships were "falling in place" in Beattie's second novel, they are "falling out of place" and fragmenting in *The Burning House.* The fragments, the dislocation, the awareness that things will not stay in place and relationships will not cohere, inform the artistic

perspective of *The Burning House* and give a unity of theme and purpose
to its portrayals of the disaffections, passivity, and sorrows of contemporary existence.

"The Burning House"

The sense of "off-balance lives slipping out of control" is captured
convincingly in the title story "The Burning House." The story focuses
upon the relationships existing amongst a group of friends; as always
in Beattie's fiction, there is the story that takes place at the surface
level and the other more significant and moving story that takes place
beneath the surface or at the edge of the narration.

In "The Burning House," the story beneath the surface concerns the
relationship of Amy and Frank Wayne, with a specific focus upon
Amy's inner states of consciousness as she watches and participates in
the relationships of her friends. Amy's confidante in "The Burning
House" is Freddy Fox, nicknamed "Reddy Fox" by Frank.

Freddy is Frank's half-brother, and Amy notes that "Freddy is closer
to me than to Frank. Since Frank talks to Freddy more than he talks
to me, however, and since Freddy is totally loyal, Freddy always knows
more than I know" (240). This sense of Amy's being left somewhat in
the dark and only sensing what she needs to know is a major theme of
the story, and one reenforced by the story's structure, in which Amy
"hovers in her kitchen like a mere eavesdropper to all the voices ad-
dressing her."[5]

As the story begins, Amy is cooking and preparing to entertain her
husband's friends for the weekend. Frank is an accountant, and Tucker,
one of his clients, is visiting, along with Freddy. Frank is in the living
room discussing art with Tucker, who owns a gallery, and Freddy is in
the kitchen helping Amy. Freddy used to work for Tucker at this gallery, but Tucker eventually had to dismiss him because Freddy regularly came to work stoned and "might say just *anything* to a customer."[6]

When the four sit down to eat, Freddy continues to get stoned, and
Frank and Tucker continue discussing art. Freddy lightheartedly refers
to his homosexuality and comments, "I keep thinking of this table as
a big boat, with dishes and glasses rocking on it" (242). Freddy goes
into the kitchen to give the dog a bone, and Frank says of Freddy, "He
should have finished school. He'll knock around a while longer, and
then get tired of it and settle down to something" (243).

In the story's next scene, Freddy and Amy are sitting on a concrete bench outdoors in an area that is a garden in the spring. They are discussing Frank's girlfriend. Freddy says little directly, but is surprised that Amy knows. "How did you find out?" he says. "He talked about her. I kept hearing her name for months, and then we went to a party at Garner's, and she was there, and when I said something about her later he said, 'Natalie who?' It was much too obvious. It gave the whole thing away" (243–44).

Freddy talks of the avocado seed he has planted outside. Amy says of Frank: "He's embarrassed. . . . When he's home, he avoids me. But it's rotten to avoid Mark, too. Six years old, and he calls up his friend Neal to hint that he wants to go over there. He doesn't do that when we're here alone" (244).

When Freddy and Amy go back inside, Amy washes dishes and Freddy dries them. Looking up, Amy screams and breaks a glass against the kitchen faucet. Too late, she realizes that the frightening apparition she saw at the kitchen window is her friend, J. D., wearing a goat mask. It has been raining heavily and J. D. is soaking wet as he enters the kitchen. He has gotten lost and driven for miles through the country before finding the house. "I'm sorry," he says, looking at Amy's badly cut finger. "I thought you'd know it was me" (246).

While Freddy and J. D. tend to Amy's cut, Marilyn, Neal's mother, calls to say that Mark does not want to spend the night and wants to come back home to Amy's.

"He's not upset now, is he?" [Amy asks].
"No, but he's dropped enough hints that he doesn't think he can make it through the night."
"O.K.," [Amy says]. "I'm sorry about all of this."
"Six years old," Marilyn says. "Wait till he grows up and gets that feeling." (248)

The phone rings again, and it is Johnny. J. D. comes down from upstairs with two Band-Aids for Amy's hand. J. D. knows of Johnny, but Amy is worried about who else might overhear. Amy ostensibly talks about a delivery late in the afternoon. "Everything is fine," she says. "'Nothing is fine,' Johnny says. 'Take care of yourself'" (249).

J. D. had introduced Amy to Johnny in the faculty lounge, where Amy had gone to get a cup of coffee after registering for classes at the university. J. D. was Frank's adviser in college. When Johnny entered the lounge, J. D. introduced Amy as Frank Wayne's wife. Later, Amy remembers: "J. D. told me he knew it the instant Johnny walked into the room—he knew that second that he should introduce me as somebody's wife. He could have predicted it all from the way Johnny looked at me" (251).

For along time, J. D. takes a great deal of pride in believing that he was prepared for what would happen next—that Johnny and Amy would get involved. But, as Amy says, "It took me to disturb his pleasure in himself—me, crying hysterically on the phone last month, not knowing what to do, what move to make next."

"Don't do anything for awhile. I guess that's my advice," J. D. says. "But you probably shouldn't listen to me. All I can do myself is run away, hide out. I'm not the learned professor. You know what I believe. I believe all that wicked fairy-tale crap: your heart will break, your house will burn" (251–52).

Later that night, after the dishes have been washed and the guests suitably entertained, Amy is lying in bed waiting for Frank to come out of the bathroom and looking at "about twenty small prisms hung with fishing line from one of the exposed beams" (252). She thinks: "I have known everybody in the house for years, and as time goes by I know them all less and less" (253). She recalls individual moments with Freddy, Tucker, and J. D.: "All those moments and all they meant was that I was fooled into thinking I knew these people because I knew the small things, the personal things" (254). Frank is even harder to understand: "One night a week or so ago, I thought we were really attuned to each other, communicating by telepathic waves, and as I lay in bed about to speak I realized that the vibrations really existed: they were him, snoring. Now he's coming into the bedroom, and I'm trying again to think what to say. Or ask. Or do" (255).

Frank tells Amy that there's a hurricane about to hit Key West and that Tucker asked a travel agent where he could pan for gold, and she told him. "Did you decide what you're going to do after Mark's birthday?" Amy says. Frank doesn't answer. Amy touches his side. "It's two o'clock in the morning. Let's talk about it another time." "You picked the house, Frank. They're your friends downstairs. I used to be what you wanted me to be. . . . I want to know if you're staying or going."

Everything you've done is commendable. You did the right thing to go back to school. You tried to do the right thing by finding yourself a normal friend like Marilyn. But your whole life you've made one mistake—you've surrounded yourself with men. Let me tell you something. All men—if they're crazy, like Tucker, if they're gay as the Queen of the May, like Reddy Fox, even if they're just six years old—I'm going to tell you something about them. Men think they're Spider-Man and Buck Rogers and Superman. You know what we all feel inside that you don't feel? That we're going to the stars.

Frank takes Amy's hand and says, "I'm looking down on all of this from space. I'm already gone" (256).

"The Burning House" is a conventional narrative—the action progresses chronologically and sequentially, with only occasional flashbacks. Characters are presented and developed, and tensions and conflicts within the story are established. But the power of "The Burning House" does not derive from conventional narration or from any aspect of plot development. Its power resides in Ann Beattie's gift for the telling detail and in her great capacity for insight into human motivations and human consciousness. Beattie has commented that a number of her stories that are otherwise different have a common focus on relationships in the process of breaking down. Her predominant focus in these stories is upon characters "who can't break away from the situation they find themselves in . . . this whole Beckettian thing—I can't stay and I can't go. This tug interests me more than the fact that they're not communicating—I want to find out why they're staying and not going."[7]

"The Burning House" can be viewed as both a representation of and an investigation of Amy's emotional stasis—exploring why she chooses to stay with Frank, waiting for his decision whether he will stay or leave; why she places her feelings for Johnny on hold while she decides about Frank; why, when she knows that, as in the fairy tales, her house is burning, she responds with an overly calm, seemingly dispassionate self-control. The image of Amy's emotional restraint is a chilling one, even in the midst of "the burning house" that once was her life with Frank. Frank has a lover; Amy will perhaps take Johnny as her lover. Mark does not want to stay in the house with his father but is afraid to be away on his own. The structure and meaning of the relationship is disintegrating, but a guest, a casual observer, would view the relationship as one of domestic stability and bliss, with Amy in the kitchen preparing a meal for guests while her husband discusses contemporary art with one of his business clients. What is *not* talked about in "The Burning House" is the most chilling aspect of the story—Frank's involvement with Natalie; Amy's attraction to Johnny; Tucker's fascination with homosexuality; Freddy's staying stoned and lost because he cannot find a direction for his life; J. D.'s quitting his job as an English professor and not doing anything with his life because his wife and son were killed in a traffic accident; J. D.'s thinking he is prepared for anything, now that he has lost his family, and everyone's knowing that J. D. isn't prepared for anything at all.

The metaphor in the story, for what is not talked about, is silence, and the metaphor for the emotional distance created by silence is space. When Amy is physically with her friends, she still feels separated from them. When she is upstairs in the bedroom, physically removed from her friends, she feels that she knows them less and less. Lying next to Frank in bed, physically close but light-years away from him emotionally, she asks if he is going to stay or go, and finds that he is already gone. He is gone, he tells her, because she, like all women, does not understand men, even though she has spent her life around them. Men are different from women in that men want to go to the stars. Women are earthbound, weighted, and tied. Men are weightless and free, free like larger-than-life comic book heroes to go to the stars and be rid of all on earth that would hold or contain them. She has misjudged and misunderstood him, Frank tells Amy; while she thought he was with her, he was already gone, following his natural destiny to be free. From space, she looks small, and insignificant, and easy to discard. She is in "the burning house," and he is drifting in space, free of the chaos and the debris.

Sanford Pinsker claims that all the stories in *The Burning House* are set in a "nether land somewhere between memories that cannot be recaptured and desires that cannot be articulated."[8] Unable to recapture her earlier relationship with Frank and unable to articulate what she needs from him in a way that he can understand, Amy is trapped in a "nether land" of passivity and sadness, watching her husband drift free, casting her away as he goes.

"Learning to Fall"

The sense of events and relationships out of control and balance that pervades "The Burning House" is also apparent in "Learning to Fall." The narrator, an unnamed woman, has come to her friend Ruth's house to take Ruth's eight-year-old son, Andrew, on a train ride into New York City. Once or twice a month the narrator and Andrew take the train from Connecticut into the city to look at shops and go to the museums. The woman does this as a favor for Ruth, so that Ruth can have some time with her lover, Brandon, and because Andrew has no friends his own age.

Looking at Andrew on their way to New York, the woman remembers the night he was born. She held Ruth's hand, comforting her, recalling that "I couldn't stop myself from grasping her wrist, the middle of her arm, hanging on to her elbow, as if she were drowning. It was the same thing I would do with the man who became my lover, years later—but then it would be because I was sinking" (5).

Ruth wanted the child, "although the man who was the father begged her to have an abortion and finally left her six months before Andrew was born" (4–5). When there was difficulty with Andrew's birth, "an impatient doctor used forceps and tugged him out, and there was slight brain damage. That and some small paralysis of his face, at the mouth" (5). One of the few times Ruth ever complained, she said to the narrator, shortly after Andrew's birth, "I'll tell you what I'm sick of. I'm sick of hearing how things might have been worse, when they might also have been better. I'm sick of lawyers saying to wait—not to settle until we're sure how much damage has been done. They talk about damage with their vague regret, the way the weatherman talks about another three inches of snow. I'm sick of wind whistling through the house when it could be warm and dry." The narrator asks Ruth if she is angry because Andrew's father has had no contact with her since before Andrew's birth. "Angry?" Ruth says. "I'm angry at myself. I don't often misjudge people that way" (10).

On the train the narrator thinks of Ruth, waiting for Brandon to come over. It is Wednesday, and Ruth does not have to go to work at the community college where she teaches. The narrator thinks: "I envy him an afternoon with Ruth, because she will cook for him and make him laugh and ask nothing from him" (9). For Valentine's Day, Brandon gave Ruth a plant with heart-shaped leaves. "If I were a poet," the narrator thinks, "those green leaves would be envy, closing her in. Like many people, he does envy her. He would like to be her, but he does not want to take her on. Or Andrew" (9).

Ruth is developed in the story as a kind and sensitive woman who is extremely loving, and who asks nothing for herself. She loved Andrew's father, who abandoned her, and she loves Brandon, who is not willing to marry her. The image of Ruth in the story is a poignant one, for she has more love to give than those around her are willing to receive.

In contrast to Ruth, the narrator is seeking not to express her emotions, but to hold them in check. She has a lover, Ray, but she is trying to break off their relationship. She has brought Andrew with her to New York partly for Ruth and Andrew's sake, and mostly to protect her from having to deal with Ray directly. The narrator's marriage to Arthur is beginning to come apart, and she has become involved with Ray out of loneliness and a strong dislike for Arthur. Now she has found, however, that "loving Ray made me as confused as disliking Arthur, and that he had too much power over me and that I could not be his lover anymore" (13). Just as she is about to take the commuter train back to Connecticut, she calls Ray. He asks if he can come buy her a drink, and she agrees.

Ray, the narrator, and Andrew sit in Grand Central Station. Ray is very kind to Andrew and talks to him of his day. Ray asks the narrator if she will stay in town and go to the ballet with him. He can get tickets for Andrew and her. She tells him that she has to go home and cook dinner for Arthur. Andrew tells Ray that his mother is learning to fall. It's an exercise in a dance class, the narrator explains. The narrator imagines Ruth "bringing her arms in front of her, head bent, an almost penitential position, and then a loosening in the knees, a slow folding downward" (14).

Ray asks the narrator to take a walk with him. She holds a large envelope she is carrying with both hands, making it obvious to Ray that she does not want to hold his hand. Ray moves in closer and puts his arm around her shoulder. "No hand-swinging like children—the proper gentleman and the lady out for a stroll. What Ruth has known all along: what will happen can't be stopped. Aim for grace" (15).

Dean Flower comments of *The Burning House,* "stories that begin in bizarre tangles of ambiguous relationships end not with explanations or solutions but usually with clarified enigmas."[9] In "Learning to Fall," we discover that "each character is locked in disappointments and failures, that fall they must, and that the only choice is whether to do so gracefully or to take another bruising. Reasonably, the narrator opts for the former." Flower also notes that "the word *grace* has no religious reverberations in Beattie's realm";[10] instead, the emphasis is upon minimal emotional survival. Those who learn to fall, who respond to the inevitable pressure of events and circumstance, become like Ruth, inured, stoic, and yet graceful and compassionate. The narrator knows that her romance with Ray is over, that this will be another fall; she leaves Ray to go home to cook dinner for a husband she no longer loves—a fall (and a failure) of another kind. Like Ruth, however, she is prepared for the fall and is aiming for grace. Certainly, echoes of

Hemingway's famous phrase "grace under pressure" abound, and clearly Beattie has in mind the same type of endurance with knowledge and fortitude that Hemingway envisions. Beattie has often been compared to Hemingway in both style and subject matter; but Flower compares her to Harold Pinter: both insist that the universe is not kind, that falls are inevitable, and that human dignity resides in accepting the consequences of failures and disappointments with strength and perseverance.

"Jacklighting"

"Jacklighting" reconsiders the theme of friendship treated most extensively by Beattie in "Friends" in *Secrets and Surprises*. Like "Friends," "Jacklighting" centers around a group of friends who have known each other for years and who have been instrumental in shaping each others' lives and identities.

The group has gathered at Spence's house to commemorate Nicholas's birthday. Nicholas, Spence's brother, was injured in a motorcycle accident and lived, brain-damaged, for almost a year before dying. This is the first year the group has been without Nicholas, and the major concern and realization everyone has is "how were we going to feel ourselves again, without Nicholas?" (23).

Although it is Nicholas's birthday, "so far no one has mentioned it" (23). Spence makes jam from berries the group has picked. He is quiet and withdrawn, almost melancholic. Spence's girlfriend, Pammy, has arrived from Washington. She is ten years younger than the others in the group and a medical student at Georgetown. She tells the narrator, who is once again an unnamed woman, that she once was a drug addict, hooked on speed. "Now she interests me," the narrator says. "I always like people who have gone through radical changes. It's snobbishness—it shows me that other people are confused, too" (24).

The characters in "Jacklighting" spend most of their time trying to recapture Nicholas's spirit and the spirit of what he meant to the group. He is described as a person who "always watched shadows." Nicholas was "the man looking to the side in Cartier-Bresson's photograph, instead of putting his eye to the wall. He'd find pennies on the sidewalk when the rest of us walked down city streets obliviously, spot the chipped finger on a mannequin flawlessly dressed, sidestep the one piece of glass among shells scattered on the shoreline. It would really have taken something powerful to do him in. So that's what happened: a drunk in a van, speeding, head-on, Nicholas out for a midnight ride without his helmet" (22). Earlier in the day, while babysitting for a neighbor's child, Nicholas had assembled "a crazy nest of treasures" in the helmet: "dried chrysanthemums, half of a robin's blue shell, a cat's-eye marble, yellow twine, a sprig of grapes, a piece of a broken ruler" (23). The helmet with its odd array of treasures is perceived by the group as a symbol of Nicholas's specialness and his irrepressible sense of wonder.

The group's gathering is going poorly. Everyone needs to talk about Nicholas's death, but no one can. "Even if he were alive," the narrator says, "I wonder if today would be anything like those birthdays of the past, or whether we'd have bogged down so hopelessly that even his childish enthusiasm would have had little effect" (25). The mood of isolation and sadness is pervasive. "Pammy says that she does not feel close to any of us—that Virginia was just a place to come to cool out. She isn't sure she wants to go on with medical school. I get depressed and think that if the birds could talk, they'd say that they didn't enjoy flying. The mountains have disappeared in the summer haze" (25).

Late that night, the narrator sits on the porch and toasts Nicholas with a glass of wine. She remembers that when she was younger she had always assumed that Nicholas would be their guide—"he was always there to excite us and to give us advice" (26). He had started a game that had gone on for years. The participants were to stare at something for a long while, close their eyes, and then envision it again. The narrator recalls, "When I closed my eyes, I squinted until the thing was lost to me. It kept going backwards into darkness" (26).

Tonight, as a tribute to Nicholas, the narrator is again closing her eyes and trying to envision something from the darkness. Her realization is that "you can look at something, close your eyes and see it again and still know nothing—like staring at the sky to figure out the distance between stars. The drunk in the van that hit Nicholas thought he had hit a deer" (26). The narrator concludes her reminiscence of Nicholas with this statement: "Tonight, stars shine over the field with the intensity of flashlights. Every year, Spence calls the state police to report that on his property, people are jacklighting" (26), a technique that hunters use to lure their prey to its death.

Daniel Zitin sees the theme of inadequate bonding as central to the meaning of "Jacklighting" and to many of Beattie's stories. "The irony of these gatherings—and of most of the social occasions Beattie presents—is that what is engendered when people get together is not closeness or understanding or love but a profound sense of the opposite. In 'Jacklighting,' the friends who meet to celebrate the dead Nicholas's birthday come to realize that he alone had held the group together"; consequently, a "feeling of ineffectuality" pervades the gathering, Zitin contends, revealing that the closeness they desire is remote, receding further and further from their grasp, just as the images they envision in their minds slip further into the darkness.[11]

There is, too, in "Jacklighting" a certain sense of tragic sorrow at the loss of innocence. Nicholas was the best among them, and, with his death, the group is lessened, spiritually and emotionally. He was, as the narrator indicates, the guide for the group, and they are more lost—both inside themselves and in the world—without his presence. He was the gentle spirit, too, the one who gathered treasures in his helmet and who could see light amidst the shadows. The circle of friends will undoubtedly open to let others in, but there is the suggestion that the newcomers will be lesser people in vision and spirit than Nicholas was. Pammy, the symbol of the new that has come to merge with the old, seems both self-centered and uninterested in the group's collective memories.

Perhaps the most powerful symbol of the loss of innocence and goodness is the image of jacklighting itself. It is a poignant and powerful image of the hunter's taking advantage of the hunted, blinding it with light so that he might lure it to its death. Nicholas is like the deer; he did not see what was coming. Blinded by his own kind of innocence and a kind of free spirit of gentleness in a world molded by callousness and insensitivity, Nicholas was "jacklighted" to his death, and left behind only images of his life and his goodness fading in the darkness.

As members of the group sit on the porch and toast Nicholas's memory, they are saluting the passing of their better days. His death is a symbol of how easily, and generally how cruelly, goodness is destroyed in this world, and often by lights coming out of the darkness that should be friendly but are not.

"The Cinderella Waltz"

Pearl K. Bell has commented that Ann Beattie's fiction "describes a wayward human landscape that is bereft of meaning, in which everyone is chronically vagrant and capricious, and unmoored,"[12] and Daniel Zitin has noted of *The Burning House* that "of the sixteen stories in this volume, almost all feature dead or disintegrating relationships."[13] In fact, the presence of "disintegrating relationships" and "unmoored" lives is so pronounced in *The Burning House* that drift and isolation, the inability of people to sustain lasting meaningful relationships, might well be perceived as the volume's central theme.

"The Cinderella Waltz" exemplifies this focus on love's dissipation by drawing upon the concept of fairy tales and happy endings to reveal the emptiness of the contemporary image of love. The story shows the romantic promise of everlasting love to be false, asserting instead the truth of Jean-Paul Sartre's statement "all promises are lies."

"The Cinderella Waltz" begins with a scene that seems conventional and typical on the surface. Nine-year-old Louise is getting ready to be picked up by her father, Milo, to spend the weekend with him. She and her mother, the narrator, are busily packing up Louise's trove of special objects, and Louise is as engrossed in her duties as her mother is anxious about the fact that Milo does not like Louise to bring much along because it only means more objects to worry about packing up when it is time for Louise to leave. Milo is a perfectionist, the narrator states. Later, she redefines his perfectionism as a desire to have everyone do things his way.

Milo and Bradley arrive to pick up Louise; Bradley is Milo's male lover, the person for whom Milo has left and divorced the narrator. "It would be an understatement to say that I disliked Bradley at first," the narrator says (44). The last year Milo was with them, the narrator says, she used to go into Louise's room "to tuck her in and tell her that everything was all right. What that meant was that there had not been a fight. . . . Then I would go downstairs and hope that Milo would say the same thing to me. What he finally did say one night was 'You might as well find out from me as some other way'" (48–49).

When they were first married, Milo and the narrator lived in an apartment in New York and moved when Louise was two years old. "When we moved, Milo kept the apartment and sublet it—a sign that things were not going well, if I had been one to heed such a warning" (58). When the story begins, Milo and Bradley live in the apartment, and the narrator is surprised to discover that she feels closer to Bradley than to Milo. Bradley works for an advertising agency, and the narrator calls him to check about freelance work. Soon, however, the calls relate less and less to business; what Bradley and the narrator discuss and, what they share in common, is Milo. Milo, and a deep concern for Louise's welfare.

The relationship among the three goes well until Bradley loses his job. Milo feels Bradley has purposefully done poorly so that he will get fired and have an excuse to leave him. Milo unleashes sarcasm and disparaging remarks upon Bradley, prompting the narrator to inquire, "Do you say anything encouraging to him about finding a job, or do you just take it out on him that he was fired?" (57). There is a pause, and then Milo "almost seems to lose his mind with impatience," telling the narrator that he doesn't appreciate "being subjected, by telephone, to an unflattering psychological analysis by my ex-wife" (57).

One of the interesting dimensions of the "The Cinderella Waltz" is that the narrator, who did not want Milo to leave her and who was devastated when he did, is cast in the role of mediator when Milo and Bradley's relationship is suffering obvious difficulties. She exhibits patience and caring, and is genuinely concerned that the two men resolve their differences—a very understanding attitude for her to possess, in view of the complexities of the situation. As she herself phrases it, "Bradley had won and I had lost" (45), but the woman distinguishes herself not by her hatred and bitterness, as might be expected, but by her loving and forgiving nature. As such, she stands in direct psychological and thematic contrast to Milo, whose self-centeredness and petty perfectionism make him arrogant and overbearing. Sarcasm is his defensive weapon, and even Louise, who adores him, is not safe from his attacks.

Louise is an interesting character within the panoply of Beattie's depictions of children. Generally, Beattie's children are worldly-wise in a negative way, like Parker, Mary, and John Joel in *Falling in Place* and Wally in the short story "Wally Whistles Dixie" in *Distortions.* Their knowledge of the world has made them either withdrawn or rebellious, and, like their adult counterparts, they are often unable to make sense of the world. Louise, however, possesses adultlike knowledge without taking on the ennui and despair of adulthood. She is precocious for a nine-year-old, carrying around a copy of Samuel Beckett's *Happy Days* and excelling in everything at school except math. She is smart enough to know that she cannot invite her friends over to her father's apartment, and also wise enough to sense that there is only so much she can let her mother know she knows. Viewing Louise, her mother recalls her own childhood—how she longed to be a tree surgeon and would stand with a stethoscope pressed to a tree trunk, listening for a heart beat. "Was my persistence willfullness, or belief in magic?" (53) she wonders, and comments that "children seem older now" (52).

Louise goes regularly to Milo and Bradley's apartment and does not

suspect that her father wants to move to San Francisco. Her father
vaguely mentions, every now and then, a desire to leave New York,
but her mother carefully guides the conversation away from the subject
to keep from upsetting Louise. In the story's conclusion, Milo has decided to move to San Francisco and breaks the news heartlessly to
Louise. He invites Louise and her mother over on the pretense of taking
them out to a Sunday brunch. At the apartment, he pours them all a
glass of champagne. "This is a toast to me," Milo says, "because I am
going to be going to San Francisco" (60). Louise bursts into tears and
runs into the bedroom.

"Everybody lets me know just what my insufficiencies are, don't
they?" Milo says. "Nobody minds expressing himself. We have it all
right out in the open" (61). Bradley indicates that Milo is mad at him
because he was offered a job in New York and did not automatically
refuse it. "You're going with him?" the narrator says. "To San Francisco?" Bradley shrugs and won't look at the narrator. "I'm not quite sure
I'm wanted" (60).

The narrator tells Milo to go in and say something to Louise. Milo
glares at her and stomps into the bedroom. She can hear him speaking
to Louise reassuringly, telling her that she can come visit him often.
Louise screams that Milo lied, that he said he was going to take them
to brunch, that he had said nothing about San Francisco. Milo again
tries to reassure her that they will still see each other often. "Louise is
sobbing. She has told him the truth and she knows it is futile to go
on" (61).

"By the next morning," the narrator says, "Louise acts the way I
acted—as if everything were just the same" (61). They all go to brunch
on Sunday morning, just as Milo has planned. Milo tells Louise to
come with him for a minute, across the street to the park, so they can
dance and so Bradley and the narrator can have a quiet drink together.
"I have hardly slept at all, and having a drink is not going to clear my
head," the narrator says. "I have to think of things to say to Louise,
later on the ride home" (62).

The narrator looks at Bradley with compassionate interest. "Why
are you going, Bradley?" the narrator says. "You've seen the way he
acts. You know that when you get out there he'll pull something on
you. Take the job and stay here" (62). Bradley pats the narrator's hand
on his arm. "Then he says the thing that has always been between us,
the thing too painful for me to envision or think about. 'I love him,'
Bradley whispers" (62–63).

When Milo and Louise return, Louise is pretending to be a young child, almost a baby, and the narrator wonders for an instant "if Milo and Bradley and I haven't been playing house, too—pretending to be adults" (63). Louise announces that Daddy is going to give her a first-class ticket and that they are going to ride in a glass elevator to the top of the Fairmont Hotel. "Before Louise was born," the narrator remembers, "Milo used to put his ear to my stomach and say that if the baby turned out to be a girl he would put her into glass slippers instead of bootees. Now he is the prince once again. I see them in a glass elevator, not long from now, going up and up, with the people below getting smaller and smaller, until they disappear" (63).

The image is one of enchantment achieved at the cost of irresponsibility. Milo is the type who leaves people behind, leaving them so quickly emotionally that they do get "smaller and smaller, until they disappear." He left the narrator for Bradley, and, as the narrator warns, he will probably leave Bradley—and leave him in such a fashion that he will make it appear to be Bradley's fault. Milo is the prince, promising the fairy-tale vision of enchanting and lasting love. He places the glass slipper on the foot of his chosen, and the chosen believes that the dance, "the Cinderella waltz," will go on forever. Fairy tales end that way, but fairy tales are for children. Louise is lost in the enchantment of the fairy tale image her father is promising: that they will be together, unchanged, in a glass tower protected from the world. The narrator, as an adult, sees that fairy tales are illusions and that, always, the dance must end. She knows that she must keep a clear head and think of what to say to Louise on the ride home—after the spell is broken and reality sets in. She was once the princess, the Cinderella, whom Milo loved, and she knows the pain of abandonment that Louise will soon come to experience.

The narrator is aware of the midnight that awaits, and the sadness of the story's ending is that she is unable to protect anyone with her knowledge. Louise is pretending, preferring the shelter of illusions and purposeful self-deception to the pain of knowing that her father is abandoning her and leaving behind only empty promises in his stead. Bradley knows the truth, seeing Milo clearly for the insensitive, self-centered manipulator he is; yet, Bradley prefers, too, to believe that love can protect him. The irony, of course, is that the narrator believed the same thing, that her love for Milo would be strong enough to make him want to stay forever. From sad experience, the narrator knows that Milo is the prince in the glass tower, the creator of fantasies and enchantments, who can invite those he loves into his magical world and, just as easily and insensitively, shut them out. Louise can dance "the Cinderella waltz" with Milo because she is still a child and innocent enough to want to believe; the narrator, however, knows that "the Cinderella waltz" is only for children. Disillusionment awaits as surely as midnight and the ride home ahead. Just as Milo will withdraw from those he loves, going further and further away emotionally until those around him disappear, the narrator will be there for those left behind— to comfort, to nurture, and to help them weather the reality that will be far less appealing and far more painful than the illusory, magical tale of enduring love that Milo has created.

The ride to the top of the glass tower Milo promises may be enchanting and delightful in its ascent, but the narrator knows that, after the illusions have worn off, the ride home is a painful and lonely journey.

"Desire"

"The Cinderella Waltz" is a story about characters on the verge of displacement. Marital and family relationships have been disrupted, and even the love relationship between Milo and Bradley is threatened by Milo's inability to content himself with any person or situation he perceives as less than perfect. The disruption, yet to come, of lives and relationships in "The Cinderella Waltz" is only hinted at—part of the story "at the boundary" that Beattie suggests with each of her narratives but does not detail.

In "Desire," the disruption has already occurred, and the primary focus of the story is upon depicting the emptiness and sadness of lost relationships. The sorrow of loss surrounds B. B., the narrator of "Desire," like a penumbra, and part of his conflict in the story is to come to terms with, to focus clearly upon, how the loss of illusions and the loss of his marriage have affected his life.

B. B. was married to Robin; they have an eight-year-old son, Bryce. Bryce lives in Vermont with Robin and with his stepsister Maddy, but he has called to invite himself to his father's house in Pennsylvania for Bryce's spring vacation.

As the story opens, Bryce is sitting at the kitchen table in B. B.'s house, cutting out a picture of Times Square. "It was a picture from a coloring book, but Bryce wasn't interested in coloring; he just wanted to cut out pictures so he could see what they looked like outside the book" (147). The image introduces a major theme of the story, that of perspective, particularly the concept of how people look outside their backgrounds or environments. Within the customary frame and background, the figures in Times Square look as if they belong; they blend in and create a clearly focused image of life. Removed from their background, they seem out of place, larger than life in their disruption and displacement. The image of figures cut out from life and made larger and more particular in their isolation is an apt metaphor for B. B., who has not yet fully understood his divorce from Robin, his new relationship with his son, or his relationship with his lover, Rona. B. B. is a person trying to see himself and to keep himself in perspective; the image he once had of reality has been shattered, and he must rebuild another image he can both believe in and embrace.

As B. B. sits at the kitchen table watching Bryce cutting out pictures, Beattie focuses the reader's attention upon two aspects of B. B. and Bryce's relationship. The first is that Bryce is much more like an adult in the conversation with his father than a child. Had the story not introduced Bryce as B. B.'s son, one observing and listening to the conversation between the two would assume that Bryce was one of B. B.'s friends. One might also note that B. B. does not know how to relate to his son, who remains a puzzlement to him. As B. B. says, when Bryce is in Vermont he is always calling B. B. to come visit him, and when Bryce is in Pennsylvania he is always calling Maddy to tell her he misses her and wishes he were at home. Bryce seems not to feel fully at home in either location, and his displacement is indicative of the emotional disruptions in his life as well as of those his father is going through.

B. B. discusses his relationship with Bryce with Rona. Rona is taking a bath, and B. B. is explaining how distanced he feels from Bryce. B. B. has bought a toy fish for Rona; it circulates in the bathtub as B. B. talks, snapping its jaws and moving through the soap bubbles. B. B. recalls how Rona used to stay stoned all the time and everything seemed funny to her—especially Bryce's children's books with pictures of flying elephants. B. B. realizes that, even though he did not get stoned with Rona, sometimes things in his life had seemed odd to him, too. He remembers vividly the time Rona's mother had sent her a loofah for Christmas and B. B. and six of his friends had crammed into the bathroom, "cheering as the floating loofah expanded in the water" (152). Again, the metaphoric image is of things taking shape and unfolding, of things coming into perspective as they unfold; in a sense, the image is an excellent symbol of the story's narrative technique, as well as an emblem for B. B.'s desire to get the events of his life in focus so that he might see what is revealed.

B. B. decides to take Bryce and Rona to a local auction held in a barn, largely because there is nothing on TV and nothing for Bryce to do. When Bryce stands up to see, B. B. notices that the metal folding chair Bryce had been sitting on has "PAM LOVES DAVID FOREVER AND FOR ALL TIME" written on it with Magic Marker. Bryce takes off his scarf and folds it over the writing (153).

Bryce wanders off, and B. B. expects to see him by the hotdog stand. Instead, he is over by a teenage boy, inspecting a box of puppies. The boy is letting Bryce hold a puppy for a dime. For a quarter, he will let Bryce hold the puppy until the auction is over. B. B. is amazed. The image of the expanding loofah comes to his mind and the time when, as a boy, he watched a neighbor drown a litter of kittens in a washtub. After the drowning, there had been a funeral. B. B., the neighbor's son, and another boy who was an exchange student had attended. The neighbor's wife had come out of the house, carrying the mother cat, and had reached in her pocket for a handful of little American flags on toothpicks to give to each of the boys; then she had gone back in the house. Ceremoniously, the neighbor had put the kittens in a shoebox coffin and buried them under an abelia bush. B. B. remembers that "the flags were what they used to give you in your sundae at the ice cream parlor next to the bank" (154).

B. B. and Rona purchase a lamp at the auction and put it on their bedside table. Rona senses that there is something wrong with B. B. "Actually," B. B. says, holding on to the window ledge, "I feel very out of control" (155).

B. B. goes downstairs. Bryce is in the dining room, drawing a picture and writing upon it with a felt pen. When B. B. asks Bryce about the picture, Bryce covers up the writing with his hands. B. B. tells Bryce that he doesn't have to show the drawing to him because he doesn't read other people's mail. Bryce reminds him that he did in Burlington.

The mail B. B. had read was a letter from Robin's sister, after Robin had left B. B. and Bryce and Robin had been missing for two days. In the letter, Robin said that she did not love B. B. and that she did not love Bryce either because he looked like his father. As she expressed it: "Let spitting images spit together" (157). Robin had run off with the cook at a natural foods restaurant. The note "was written on the back of one of the restaurant's flyers, announcing the menu for the week the cook ran away. Tears streaming down his cheeks, he had stood in the spare bedroom—whatever had made him go in there?—and read the names of desserts: 'Tofu-Peach Whip!' 'Granola Raspberry Pie!' 'Macadamia Bars'!" (157).

Bryce tells B. B. that the note he is writing is make-believe anyway and wads the paper up. Bryce smoothes the sheet out and B. B. sees that it is a tender and innocent love letter. Bryce tells B. B. that it is for Maddy. "Maddy is your stepsister," B. B. says. "You're never going to be able to marry Maddy." Bryce stares at him. "You understand?" B. B. says (158). Bryce starts to cry. "She's going to be Madeline and I'm going to live with only her and have a hundred dogs." B. B. reaches out to comfort his son, and Bryce pulls away. Robin was wrong, B. B. thinks. "Bryce was the image of her, not him—the image of Robin saying, 'Leave me alone'" (158).

B. B. goes upstairs. "Rather, he went to the stairs and started to climb, thinking of Rona lying in bed in the bedroom, and somewhere not halfway to the top, adrenaline surged through his body. Things began to go out of focus, then to pulsate. He reached for the railing just in time to steady himself. In a few seconds the first awful feeling passed, and he continued to climb, pretending, as he had all his life, that this rush was the same as desire" (158–59).

Of all the stories in *The Burning House*, "Desire" seems most to emphasize enervation and displacement as the condition of the contemporary soul. B. B. is almost too emotionally exhausted to go upstairs to his lover; all that carries him up the stairs is the biochemical afterglow of an adrenaline rush, which, all his life, he has led himself into believing was the same as desire. There is nothing in his life that B. B. does desire. The emptiness of his life has come into clear focus for him in his interaction with Bryce. Bryce is entertaining an ideal image of eternal love with Maddy; like all romantics and dreamers, Bryce holds to the vision that they will be happy together and that neither of them will ever change. In interacting with Bryce, B. B. sees both the innocent absurdity of Bryce's romantic view and the sorrow and grief Bryce goes through when B. B. shatters his illusions. The pain that Bryce experiences is thematically equivalent to B. B.'s pain over the loss of Robin. There are no happy endings, love does not last, and love is no protection against pain. Seeing these truths very clearly and, for the first time in the story, having the events and the sorrows of his life in focus, B. B. has nothing left inside of him, emotionally or spiritually, to pull him toward his future. Defeated and emotionally broken, B. B. finds the only belief left to him is the hope that stoicism can take the place of desire.

Entropy and Grace

In Ann Beattie's works prior to *The Burning House,* characters express unfulfilled romantic longings, but, like Charles in *Chilly Scenes of Winter* or Robert in "Colorado," they still pursue their fantasies and draw sustenance and succor from their illusions. In *The Burning House,* illusions are heavy weights upon the souls of Beattie's characters, and such pervasive nihilism affects her characters that nothing seems worth aspiring to. Even the great ideal of romantic love has been shown to be purposeless and empty. Human relationships fail; parents either cannot ease their children's emotional pain, like B. B. in "Desire," or they purposely lie to their children, like Milo in "The Cinderella Waltz," to spare themselves further discomfort. Marriages are either already irretrievably lost or in the process of falling apart. Desire has been replaced by endurance, and even endurance seems only an empty gesture.

In each of the stories of *The Burning House,* escapism is a predominant motif. Characters, like Frank in "The Burning House," want to surge into space and leave their lovers behind, or, like Milo and Louise in "The Cinderella Waltz," want to transcend the limits of earthly desire by going up and up and away until all that is real is but an inconsequential blur. The narrator of "Afloat," a story about a disintegrating love relationship, says that there is one desire "that can be more overwhelming than love—the desire, for one brief minute, simply to get off the earth" (197). In "Girl Talk," a woman who feels somewhat out of place amongst her lover's bizarre and distant family begins to go into labor and thinks, "There is every possibility that my baby will be loved and cared for and will grow up to be like any of these people." Moments later, the reality of her situation is revealed to her as a poignant insight: "I am really at some out-of-the way beach house, with a man I am not married to and people I do not love, in labor. . . . Pain is relative" (38).

In *The Burning House,* characters admit their pain and admit their desire to escape the earth, to be free, for one moment, from the weight of earthly despair. If *Chilly Scenes of Winter* brought Beattie comparisons to J. D. Salinger and *Falling in Place* brought comparisons to John

Updike and John Cheever, perhaps Beattie's mentors for *The Burning House* were Samuel Beckett and Harold Pinter, for, in each of these writers, the poignancy of the human condition is represented by existential despair. Their characters, like Beattie's, seem to wait, to long; ironically, even in the process of waiting, they do not know what to seek or what can save them. Knowing they will fall, and knowing that pain is inevitable, they "aim for grace." In a certain sense, they wait for grace, just as they wait for desire; and, in the interim, they sustain themselves with the knowledge that "pain is relative."

Chapter Eight
Love Always
Friends and Lovers

Love Always has been described as Ann Beattie's comedy of manners.[1] Opening on the last day of June 1984 and set in the green hills of Vermont, the novel details the complex lives of a group of old friends involved in the production of a hip, postcounterculture magazine called *Country Daze,* "whose success was proof positive that the whole country was coked-out."[2]

The editor and former owner of the magazine is Hildon, the epitome of a "neo-hippie capitalist" (64) who exudes both confidence and "preppie refinement" (19). "An only child from a middle-class family who went to prep school and to Yale, dodged the draft, was admitted to law school at the University of Virginia and dropped out," Hildon regards himself as having been "in the right place at the right time; instead of the Let's-Open-a-Restaurant dream, he had started a magazine and put lots of his friends to work. He saw the magazine as an extended family, a continuation of the life he and his friends had led in college. Obviously, they were beating the system, and while he didn't think he or this bunch was representative, he was sure that they all felt very lucky and grateful" (49).

Hildon is married to Maureen, a socialite who prides herself upon giving perfect parties to celebrate *Country Daze*'s success. Each party has had a motif; Maureen "decided on clever parties so that she, at least, would be amused" (3). This year's theme is the sea, and Maureen has filled the party scene with assorted ocean paraphernalia. She is wearing a sarong "tied tightly at her hipbone"; the wine is Entre-Deux-Mers, and a record of ocean sounds is playing in the background. Maureen wears a blue barette in the shape of a starfish (3–4).

The first of the guests to arrive is Matt Smith, to whom Hildon has sold *Country Daze* at a handsome profit. As the new owner and publisher of the magazine, Matt is immersed in the rhetoric of the self-reliant American capitalist. "I discriminate enough to know who means most to me," he says. "I always did say that a man has to know how to play his cards in this world, and sometimes he'd better realize that the best game is solitaire" (4). For Matt, Maureen flashes "her best summer smile" (4).

The most dramatic entrance to the party is made by Lucy Spenser, who, as Cindi Coeur, "a Latter-Day Miss Lonelyhearts," writes the advice to the lovelorn column for *Country Daze*. Maureen is jealous of Lucy because "everything Lucy wore and did was perfect" (4). She is also jealous because Lucy and Hildon, who have been lovers since college, are continuing their affair. Lucy sees Maureen and lights up with "a flawlessly false smile" (4). Maureen thinks, "Lucy shimmered. She acted like that woman, whatever her name was, whom *The Great Gatsby* had been in love with" (5).

The reference in *Love Always* to *The Great Gatsby* is both enticing and thematically apt, for, in many ways, *Love Always* can be viewed as *The Great Gatsby* in contemporary dress because of its focus upon the decadence that underlies the veneer of affluence and success in contemporary society. The shallowness of contemporary society is the major theme of *Love Always,* just as the superficiality and moral enervation of society in the twenties generated the focus of *The Great Gatsby.* If Lucy can be analogously compared to Daisy Buchanan, Hildon can be viewed as a diminished Jay Gatsby—a type of Gatsby manqué, in essence—for Hildon has embraced the American dream of materialism and conspicuous consumption without also embracing a Platonic image of a higher self or of undying romantic love.

Like Fitzgerald's characters, the characters of *Love Always* are careless people, too. "A rarefied group of hippies turned yuppies,"[3] they epitomize "newly affluent Baby Boomers"[4] whose wealth serves as a cover for a lack of self-definition and purpose in their lives. As they move from party to party, love affair to love affair, they tellingly represent "the new lost generation" in search of something more meaningful in life than compiling "a magazine of smart swipes"[5] and videotaping their backyard parties.

Love Letters

Lucy, as the Miss Lonelyhearts of her era, represents the period's accumulated wisdom on life and love. Ironically, "Lucy invents the anguished letters as well as her unhelpful replies," and "her column's success derives from its campy irrelevancy."[6] Maureen describes Lucy's column as "exactly the right endeavor for the society girl who wanted to stay sour" (4), and "Lucy herself admitted to a morbid fascination with being facile" (11). "Determinedly unserious," the staff of *Country Daze* is "professionally engaged in parodying concern for other people's problems."[7] As such, their jovial and contemptuous refusal to deal with the real issues of life reveals both their insensitivity and indifference, as well as the general shallowness of their hearts and spirits.

Beattie's worldly sophisticates conduct their search for happiness within a contemporary version of the Garden of Eden, and the contrast in the novel between sophistication and innocence is a pronounced one. The pastoral setting of *Love Always* is described as idyllic; "Vermont really was a paradise in a way. . . . It was more beautiful than any invented backdrop, a sky against which Lassie could be painted, noble and romantic, with wind-fluffed fur" (15).

Beattie's comic description, detailed through images of television and the movies that only further emphasize the absurd reality of contemporary existence, provides a perfect setting for Lucy's niece, fourteen-year-old Nicole Nelson. "A precocious celebrity,"[8] Nicole plays Stephanie Sykes, an abused, alcoholic teenager on America's favorite soap opera, *Passionate Intensity*. Jane, Nicole's mother and Lucy's sister, has called to ask if Lucy will take Nicole for the summer, so that Nicole can rest before her television series begins filming again, and so that Jane can have time alone with her new boyfriend. Lucy is not sure that Vermont in the summer is what Nicole needs. "You know what happens here?" Lucy says. "In the late afternoon the cows walk into the field." "Boredom might be good for her," Jane says. "Don't people develop their imaginations if they're bored?" "Why argue? Lucy thought. If Jane had made up her mind, the visit from Nicole was a *fait accompli*. Only seconds elapsed before Jane's ideas materialized. Their mother likened Jane's mind to a dollop of pancake batter dropped on a hot griddle" (13).

That Jane should see a summer in the country as a peaceful refuge for Nicole is ironic, in view of the fact that Lucy is also seeking refuge in Vermont from the loss of her relationship with Les Whitehall. Les is described in *Love Always* as the consummate yuppie, the ultimate in suave, self-centered, materialistic sophistication. Hildon despises Les because Lucy was in love with him, and Les regards Hildon as a shallow hypocrite. As hip and above-it-all as Lucy pretends to be in dispensing advice to her readers on how to reduce personal problems to the simplest terms, "since Les had taken off, she hadn't figured out how to get her life going again. It was not that the two of them had had specific plans that had been interrupted, but that when he left she realized that she had lived so long without thinking of the future that now it was difficult to imagine what she should do" (10). Les has been gone for a year, yet Lucy's mailbox is still marked Spenser/Whitehall. Wrapped in self-delusions himself, Les, nonetheless, sees Lucy's self-imposed retreat from reality for what it is and wants Lucy to see herself and her situation clearly. He writes a letter to Lucy in her capacity as Cindi Coeur, in which he urges her to abandon her protective environment and risk being herself:

Dear Cindi Coeur
My problem is my former lover. She writes an advice column for messed-up people, but the joke is, she is very messed up herself. She has never broken the tie—or made a real connection—with the man who is now her boss and longtime on-again, off-again lover. Years ago, I thought that if we left New York and moved to Vermont, they could confront the situation (Vermont is also where he is in hiding from being a serious person) and find out for themselves what was real and what was a delusion. Are they hedonists or masochists? Nothing has made them figure it out, including my leaving. Don't you miss me? Aren't you tired of avoiding yourself and of parodying somebody who does care about people's problems? Now that you don't have me to analyze anymore, have you spent any time trying to figure yourself out? I'll tell you one thing: you're a hard act to follow. Can we see each other?

Love Always,
Les   (56).

The letter from Les to Cindi Coeur is both an intriguing and ironic narrative technique in *Love Always*. Les signs the letter with "love always," raising a central question in the novel of the durability of love in the modern world. Les promises "love always," yet he has left Lucy and seems to be in retreat from any serious emotional involvements. Ironically, the letter is addressed to Lucy's persona, yet it encourages Lucy to be genuine and vulnerable as a person, open to the insights and self-discoveries she needs to abandon false pretenses and find her true purpose in life. Similarly, the letter points out a major theme of the novel in Les's statement that Hildon "is in hiding from being a serious person," and, by implication, so is Lucy. From Beattie's perspective, all the characters in *Love Always* are in hiding from being serious, purposeful human beings, and all are in need of exposing. As the novel unfolds, the unmasking of each character is a primary emphasis as well as a nexus to the insights that free several of the characters toward self-definition. And, ultimately, too, the pretenses of the characters of *Love Always* are intended to be emblematic of contemporary society. In focusing upon and revealing her characters' illusions and guises, Beattie is commenting upon, as a social satirist, the distortions affecting and defining the contemporary era.

Perhaps a deeper irony resides in the fact that the letter urging Lucy to be genuine—to come out of hiding and be who she really is—is written by a man who exists within a maze of guises and yet is charismatic and powerful enough to manipulate that maze to his advantage. Les is suave, sophisticated, and clever, a true Machiavellian spirit. The one quality Lucy admires in Les is how little he "might need or desire any closeness with other people." Lucy admits that "as crazy as it was to envy such an attitude, she did envy it, a little" in Les, "whose ability to know when to withdraw was as flawless as having perfect pitch" (114).

Despite Les's charisma and flair, Lucy sees him very clearly and knows that he has purposefully chosen his strategy of distance from others because "he thought he was out of control" (114). His philosophy is to be the one in power so that he has control over the love he gives and the degree of commitment he is willing to make. Lucy even sees Les's career in teaching as a reflection of his need to control others—in this case, a captive audience. She characterizes Les as "an intellectual shit kicker: he gave lazy paraphrases of philosophers' thoughts, pretended to think ironically of his own existence, and chose the easiest audience a coward could find—college kids" (19).

In his personal relationships, Les let others feel approved of, "but in reality he did not approve of himself or anyone else. Anyone who had less than he had wasn't worth his time, and anyone who had more was a threat. That was Les: he perceived of everything in terms of competition. He was still racing with the football, but running more slowly than he had in Carbondale, the letters on the back of his jersey replaced, when necessary, with his heart on his sleeve. The new goal was to get women" (29). In Lucy's estimation, "Les took it easy on himself. He shadowboxed until he got his equilibrium back, and if he had trouble regaining it, he bounced from one woman to another, staying on his toes" (30). His poses are stylized and almost perfect; "people who didn't know him well would be slow to spot the fear disguised as optimism" or to realize that "he wasn't achieving as much as he might" (27).

When Lucy feels that she is getting close to Les and beginning to understand him, he leaves her. In part, he says it is because Lucy has never resolved her feelings for Hildon, and, in part, it is because Les is afraid of commitments. This inability of characters to connect on any meaningful level is an important aspect of the thematic structure of *Love Always* in that none of the major characters has a love relationship of any depth or permanency. Les and Lucy have separated, and Lucy is involved on an intermittent basis with Hildon. Hildon has Lucy as his lover and is also involved with Antoinette Hadley-Cooper, a wealthy socialite. Hildon's wife, Maureen, is having an affair with Matt Smith, the publisher of *Country Daze*, mostly to spite Hildon. What Maureen discovers, though, is that "doing something like that was self-destructive: she was only being spiteful to herself" (57). Sadly, this is the only modicum of insight that Maureen achieves into her own behavior; she, like many of the characters in *Love Always*, can see the limitations and destructive consequences of self-defeating behavior, but she possesses neither the insight nor the will to achieve self-fulfilling behavior. Trapped in the cycle of superficiality and insincerity that marks the characters of *Love Always*, Maureen, with her pseudoartistic and pseudoaesthetic parties and her false summer smiles, represents the spiritual entropy that Beattie envisions as at the heart of the contemporary era. Maureen, smiling falsely in the summer twilight and pursuing self-destructive affairs, symbolizes the dissipation of values and of potential that Fitzgerald and Hemingway wrote so poignantly of in describing "the lost generation" of the 1920s. "The lost generation" of the 1980s flaunts its shallowness and sadness at Hildon's parties, rather than at Gatsby's, but the spiritual decay and emptiness are still as apparent, nonetheless.

Video Daze

Relationships in *Love Always* are unclear or undefined, and the complexities of the involvements rival those of any soap opera. Indeed, Alice Hoffman comments that "the characters of 'Love Always' are defined, as they are in soap operas, not by interior complexities and perceptions, but by the role they play in others' lives and by external details."[9] Thus, it is an interesting turn of plot and theme that Beattie introduces Nicole Nelson, star of *Passionate Intensity*, into the world of *Country Daze*. The thematic implication is, of course, that one cannot distinguish between reality and soap operas today, because contemporary society is a soap opera. This blurring of the lines between illusion and reality is central to *Love Always,* as the novel focuses upon the roles people play and the acting they do to get through their days. The characters are engaged in a vast and prolonged escape from reality, and the focus upon television as the major medium of the present age brings out Beattie's insistence that pretenses distort contemporary values and definitions of the self. The technique of comparing reality with the world of fantasy and make-believe to reveal that the distinction between truth and pretense has been lost recalls a number of other contemporary novels—most especially Walker Percy's *Lancelot,* which uses the filming of a movie to point out that in the contemporary era people play roles rather than establish an existential sense of their own personhood—and serves to show not only the intensity of Beattie's social satire but the depth of her vision.

Consistent with Beattie's antiromantic vision, there is generally a character in Beattie's novels who embodies an innocent view of the world. Set in contrast to the complexities of contemporary society, the character usually undergoes a type of disillusionment, or loss of innocence, representative of the age's loss of significant values. Beattie, in fact, has commented that disillusionment is "an underlying attitude" of her fiction and a primary aspect of her world view.[10] In *Love Always,* Nicole, at fourteen, seems to be an innocent child entering into the pastoral bliss of *Country Daze.* In truth, however, she is far more sophisticated than even her Aunt Lucy realizes. In her soap-opera role as an abused, alcoholic teenager, Nicole portrays the loss of childhood innocence; her character, Stephanie Sykes, is worldly-wise, tough, cynical, and self-reliant. In her own life, Nicole manifests many of the characteristics of her soap-opera alter ego. She possesses no childhood illusions or innocence, having lost them both to the glitter of Hollywood, dream and fantasy capital of the world. Even at fourteen, she knows that the primary quality one needs to possess in the contemporary world is the ability to play the game. "You've got to figure out a way to stay on top," she is told, "whether you're a phony or a real person" (40).

When Nicole becomes involved with Edward Bartlett, a photographer, in a game to photograph Bartlett nude and send the pictures to Bartlett's girlfriend who has rejected him, Lucy chides Nicole for her overly adult behavior by pointing out to Nicole that she is only fourteen. "Come on, Lucy," Nicole responds. "That's not fair. You know nobody ever thinks about that" (104).

Nicole's statement distresses Lucy deeply. She realizes that Nicole is right; "they *didn't* think of her as a child. She was one of them, and it seemed everyone had forgotten that she had less sophistication, less resources, and sensitive feelings. Nicole had such a good act going that she had convinced all the adults" (105).

Lucy begins to see how fully Nicole's life is an enactment of a part. "Nicole, amazingly, had the sense that everything was programmed: she knew what she was supposed to do, and she did it; she knew what other people were supposed to do, and if they didn't do it, they were fired, and people who would do it were brought in. And the sad thing was, Nicole wasn't even cynical—she didn't get the mean sense of satisfaction some cynic would get from living in such a world. Nicole wasn't angry. But she also wasn't inspired. She was complacent, and Lucy found that scary" (115).

Lucy decides that she will enrich Nicole's life by getting her more involved with her friends. Nicole, however, tells Lucy that she has no friends—she only hangs out with her mother and with her agent, Piggy Proctor. When Lucy tells Nicole that she could make friends, she responds, "I don't need any more hassles. You've got to do things for friends. They jerk you around" (112). Amazed that Nicole can feel as she does, Lucy adamantly contends that deep down Nicole must really want some friends of her own. "People don't have friends when they're my age and they're in the business," [Nicole says]. "It's a thing from your generation that people have friends" (112).

Children and Adults: The Social Mirror

Apparent in *Love Always* is the "adultomorphization" of children that Joshua Gilder notes in Beattie's fiction.[11] Nicole is an adultlike child in the midst of childlike adults. Hildon, Les, Lucy, and Maureen do not want to grow up and face the adult world of responsibility, and Nicole has had growing up imposed upon her since she was literally a child. Nearly all the adults in *Love Always* (especially Hildon) are victims of the Peter Pan syndrome[12] and seek to remain children forever, while Nicole embodies the lost child within the adult. Nicole is wise enough, however, to be able to distinguish between her true identity and her posed identity as Stephanie Sykes; most of the adults in *Love Always* do not possess such wisdom and are unable to see their pretenses as pretenses. They prefer, instead, to envision their poses and self-deceptions as their true selves, and what they value most in the novel are others who will hide from the truth with them.

In Beattie's emphasis upon revealing the illusory self-images by which her characters survive in *Love Always,* it is apparent how much of the novel centers upon games and posing. At Maureen's party, guests work upon developing personas and idealized images; fake smiles are as prevalent as Polo shirts and Gucci handbags. In an advice letter in her column, Lucy writes, "What a thing is and what we can make it appear to be is very important" (16). In interacting with Lucy, Hildon is forced to see how much of their involvement is predicated upon the ritualized enactment of games.

Jealous that Lucy has flirted with a young man, Hildon finds Lucy denying responsibility for her actions through skillful rhetoric and feigned innocence. Hildon realizes "he would be old without ever having won a fight, but he would still have Lucy. . . . She wasn't going to let anybody have anything easily besides their own false assumptions." Giving in to Lucy to disarm her petulance, Hildon knows that "it was over. Another moment when he might have lost her had passed" (22). Each begins to apologize to the other for hurt feelings, and Hildon sees that they are involved in the same game they have played since they became lovers in college—each of them "belittled themselves so much that the other would be overwhelmed with positive feelings. That was the way they had so often ended up in bed." As they begin to embrace, Hildon starts to laugh. "He needed to choke back a terrible sadness that had started to overwhelm him" (25). Even the realization that he and Lucy are seldom sincere, even in their most intimate moments, is not enough to free Hildon, just as the sadness he feels at being caught up in a meaningless masquerade is not enough to keep him from acting out his role. There is some comfort to be found in falsity and perhaps none to be found in risking the truth. As a social realist, Beattie knows that for her characters, "tender is the night," and a darkness that is known will always be preferable to unfathomed light.

While many of the characters in *Love Always* are vain, pompous, and self-deceived, the Great Pretender in the novel is Andrew Steinborn, a would-be novelist and would-be F. Scott Fitzgerald. While a student in the creative writing workshop at the University of Iowa, Steinborn had written what he considered to be his masterpiece, a novel about "a talented, misunderstood man who never completed novels" (147). His latest fictive effort is *Buzz,* a novel "about people at a fashionable resort in Southhampton, as seen from the perspective of a mosquito" (147).

Steinborn is in love with Lillian Worth, a former nurse at Massachusetts General, who gave up her medical career to move to Iowa and to live with Steinborn during the last six months of his residence. "Creativity was just in the air," (147), for Lillian had written about a dozen poems while in Iowa, "and it was Andrew's idea that she might put together a book of verse for the terminally ill and dying—a realistic yet inspirational, no holds-barred book influenced by her reading of Elisabeth Kubler-Ross and her personal experience of watching people die" (147–48). Wisely, Lillian abandons her plans to become a great poet and returns to her nursing career in Massachusetts. Steinborn is to follow, as soon as his novel sells and he has enough money to marry her.

In the meantime, however, Steinborn is chosen to do the novel serialization of the daytime soap opera *Passionate Intensity.* His choice as the great chronicler of America's cultural values and interests goes to his head, making him even more pompous and insufferable. He is convinced, now, that he is living F. Scott Fitzgerald's life. In fact, he is convinced that he *is* F. Scott Fitzgerald, and he wants Lillian to go along with his fantasies. They go on a prehoneymoon before their marriage and stay at the Birches. Steinborn says that "they had been in motels before, but no place as classy as this. He felt like a child playing grown-up. . . . F. Scott Fitzgerald had felt what he was feeling now: that so much was expected when you were in a high-class, adult world. Maybe that was why he liked Zelda so much—because she cut through all that, she insisted on remaining the child. Or the *enfant terrible*" (177).

Steinborn delights in telling Lillian stories about Fitzgerald in Paris or at the Plaza, most of which Lillian has heard before. He delights in spinning fantasies of how they will live lives exactly like Fitzgerald and Zelda's. Lillian, however, is rapidly losing interest in Steinborn. She has met a man on the plane from Iowa to Massachusetts to whom she is attracted, and she finds Steinborn's overidentification with Fitzgerald tedious and childish. "I don't know how I'm going to fit into your life," she says. "I think that maybe you aren't always realistic" (182).

Steinborn's response is to dismiss her criticism and to suggest that she may prefer someone with a conservative philosophy. "But you might let yourself in for a lot of disappointment if you really have this

image of us as Scott and Zelda, living it up in New York," Lillian
continues. "I mean, I read that book you gave me. They were both
outlaws from their own lives." "They didn't fit into the slot they'd
been assigned, if that's what you mean," Steinborn says. "I don't mean
that. I mean, they were actors. And they were so ambitious. You can't
think we're anything like them." "He was very romantic, and he was
a risk taker," Steinborn responds. "Don't you see me that way?"

She did not. "But she wasn't Zelda, and it seemed cruel to say that
she thought there was a difference between being a romantic and being
a dreamer" (182–83).

Steinborn continues to press his case, urging Lillian to believe that
he will be a great writer and that their lives will be filled with fantasy
and romance. "Put me down," he says. "I deserve it. But I want you
to know that I can prove myself to you." She realizes that "he was back
to being F. Scott Fitzgerald, but suddenly it occurred to her that the
routine had never quite been what she thought it was; he wanted to
pretend that she was a bitch and *only* a bitch. Simple, like silly Zelda"
(187).

Even the deceptions one enacts, the poses and roles one adopts, have
levels upon levels of complexity. Lillian tries to be the fanciful lover
she thinks Steinborn wants, only to discover that it is another role he
is after. Despite Lillian's efforts to dissuade Steinborn from his deluded
romanticism, he remains locked in the belief that he can live Fitzgerald's life. Steinborn is his own soap opera, and that is why it is so
appropriate that he is selected to be the cultural historian who interprets the significance of *Passionate Intensity* to the world.

Steinborn goes about his task by interviewing the members of the
soap opera's cast. When he talks with Nicole, he wants her to take a
dramatic stance toward her work—to find more meaning in what she
does with her role and the ways in which she projects the emotions and
moods of her character. Nicole, however, is not on the ego trip that
Steinborn wishes; she is direct and honest, telling him that most of
what she does and how she reacts is dependent upon which of the stars
in the show is supposed to get the most lines or the most close-ups.
Steinborn, finding such a pragmatic and sincere answer hard to accept,
dismisses Nicole's response and continues to press her to examine and
discuss the deep well of emotions within her from which she draws the
energy and insight to portray her character. Again, as with Lillian,
Steinborn wants her to be something other than what she is—in essence, he wants her to become the roles he assigns her. Steinborn is

directing his cast of characters, endeavoring to make everyone he relates to an actor within the script he envisions.

As the "country days" of *Love Always* continue to progress, nearly all the characters seek a persona behind which to hide from themselves and the world. The most honest of the characters is Nicole, who is more than willing to admit that she is only enacting a role and that she has an identity separate from it. As she tells one of her admirers, who would prefer that she sustain all of his illusions by being Stephanie Sykes rather than Nicole Nelson, "A lot of me goes into my character, but other stuff goes into being me" (144). What Nicole is in the process of defining is her adulthood, and it is perhaps inevitable within the thematic framework of *Love Always* that the beginning of adulthood be associated with the break with one's past, especially the break with one's family. In Nicole's case, the separation is a tragic one. Her mother, Jane, is killed in a motorcycle accident while honeymooning with the twenty-five-year-old man she recently married.

In Jane and Nicole's relationship, the roles had been reversed. Nicole was the child who quickly became an adult, who earned the living for the family, and who shouldered adult responsibilities. Jane remained the child, pursuing her hobbies, indulging her whims, acting on impulse, and rebelling against conventions and against her own mother, Rita. Jane's death makes both Nicole and Lucy see how fragile human bonds and relationships are, as well as realize that their fragmented lives are the result of disrupted family units. Lucy reflects upon how all the people in the group have no father—real, ceremonial, or symbolic. Piggy Proctor "was as much of a father as any of them had" (214), and Piggy is himself a self-centered, egotistical adult-child.

Narcissism and the Search for Community

There is a need for bonding expressed in *Love Always,* but none of the characters seems able to find a lasting means of meeting the human need for love. As Alice Hoffman indicates, "what is going on here isn't camaraderie, it's narcissism. . . . The impact of Hollywood as a manufactured community reverberates throughout 'Love Always,' and the characters know a great deal more about movie stars than they do about one another. In part, Miss Beattie is writing about the search for, and the inability to find, a community."[13]

This focus upon the insubstantiality of human relationships is one that characterizes Beattie's fiction, from the earliest stories in *Distor-*

tions to the poignant depictions of failing love relationships in *Love Always*. In the latter work there are echoes of Beattie's assertions in *Chilly Scenes of Winter* and in "Friends" in *Secrets and Surprises* that, in contemporary society, friendship comes the closest to fulfilling the human need for bonding and belonging; yet, even in the closest of friendships, there is still the unbridged gap, the vacuum of unmet needs.

Even in the most intimate of relationships, closeness and sincerity seem impossible goals. Love relationships disintegrate into either stylized games, like Lucy and Hildon's, Steinborn and Lillian's, or casual affairs, like Myra and Edward's, Maureen and Matt's. Marriages do not prosper and survive, because of a lack of commitment, and parental bonds are insufficient because too many of the adults in *Love Always* are obsessed with acting like children. As Nigel the photographer says, "Set the camera on infinity and you're bound to get the long view" (214). The long view, in Beattie's estimation, reveals a cycle of emotional instability and need, in which childlike adults are unable to meet the needs of children, and in which those same children will spend their adulthood looking for the love and security they did not have as children. Rita speculates upon Jane and Lucy's childhood and remembers that "in Oriental rugs, there is often an irregularity in the pattern—a key, it is called—woven that way deliberately, to allow the spirit to escape" (223). Perhaps Beattie's focus in *Love Always* is upon "the key" that will break the constricting pattern of the child-to-adult-to-child syndrome and "allow the spirit to escape."

Chapter Nine

Romanticism and Neorealism: The Achievement of Ann Beattie

Ann Beattie has called critics' efforts to interpret an author's work "pretentious guesses";[1] thus, one is hesitant not only to offer analyses of Beattie's writings but to make an overall assessment of the quality of her work and to estimate her critical potential. A number of facts about Beattie's literary odyssey are known, however, from which meritorious conclusions may be drawn.

Perhaps the most significant aspect of Beattie's career is that she is a neorealist, and, as such, she is writing fiction within the most thoroughly defined and significant of literary movements. Realism has produced the most extensive tradition of any literary movement and the most extensive critical framework exists for its analysis and assessment. For these reasons it is unlikely that Beattie's work will be regarded as experimental and antitraditional and, therefore, of only passing historical interest; and it is highly likely that Beattie's critical reputation will continue to ascend as critics interested in realism begin to analyze and assess her as the leading figure in the neorealist movement in contemporary fiction.

To assert that Beattie's strong emphasis upon neorealistically recording her era will make her attractive to critics interested in assessing the contemporary period is not to neglect, however, the fact that aspects of Beattie's work may "date" her writings. Laura Mathews has commented that Beattie has the unique gift for producing novels that seem like "a history of the day before yesterday."[2] While such immediacy is obviously a strength in Beattie's neorealistic approach, it is also a potential drawback as references that are timely and clear when a novel is published become obscure and possibly trivial as their historical significance fades.

In *Love Always,* for example, one character discusses another character's wealth by indicating that he bought into Coleco "pre-Cabbage

Patch and sold pre-Adam" (41). One might wonder how well such time-specific references will hold up in twenty or twenty-five years, and how much of *Love Always*'s ascerbic humor will be lost as the significance of these esoteric, "in" jokes is lost. Similarly, one might wonder how quickly references to Jodie Foster in the movie *Taxi Driver,* or to John Belushi doing Samurai Swordsman on *Saturday Night Live* will date Beattie's fiction. In *Chilly Scenes of Winter,* references to song lyrics that were powerful determinants of the cultural milieu of the 1960s seem to lose much of their significance and impact when the novel is read or analyzed years later. Skylab and its descent from the heavens is a major motif of *Falling in Place,* but this reference, too, has the potential of reducing the universality and lasting import of Beattie's fiction.

Discussing the limitations of the time-specific references in Beattie's work is not to contend, however, that Beattie could be an effective neorealist if she did not use materials from her own era in generating the thematic and philosophical perspectives of her fiction. In fact, to argue that Beattie could be a contemporary neorealist without drawing upon her own era in her fiction seems more than a contradiction in terms. The essence of the issue is this: are there sufficient philosophical substance and literary merit to Beattie's writings to compensate for the potential limitations and drawbacks of references in her writings that depend upon an awareness of the period for their impact? On the basis of critical responses to Beattie's work, the answer is a definite "yes." And rightly so, for Beattie has done more than any other writer to redefine the neorealist movement and to influence contemporary literature away from metafiction or surfiction and toward realism.

Equally significant, Beattie has influenced the structure of neorealism by developing a highly unique and identifiable style. What has been called Beattie's "deadpan" or "emotionless" style, Beattie herself characterizes as a mode of writing that is "very mannered" and in which there is an effort to eliminate "an intrusive, editorializing narrator."[3] Undoubtedly, Beattie's style is the aspect of her work to which critics have most strongly responded; and, not surprisingly, there is a measure of debate over both the efficacy and merit of Beattie's minimalist prose style.

Joseph Epstein, for example, considers Beattie "a writer with a true command of style and a deadly eye for right details,"[4] while Whitney Balliett describes Beattie's approach to fiction as a type of "super-realism" in which Beattie "does not spend much time on exteriors—on streets and highways and landscapes. But she never misses the people who populate them."[5] In a similar vein, David Kubal states that Beattie's "aesthetic surfaces are coolly brilliant,"[6] and Jack Beatty envisions Beattie's narrative technique as "a reflective realism of accurate detail."[7] Not all critics, however, are as highly laudatory. Joshua Gilder lambasts Beattie's style as "hangdog prose"—a "stunted use of language alternating with sodden bursts of lyricism" and decries the absence of emotive projections and responses in Beattie's work.[8]

Gilder's assessment is representative of those critics who strongly dislike the affectless quality of Beattie's style and who would prefer, instead, a type of emotionally infused, imagistic style with sincerity as its base, and metaphor as its essential device. At issue, here, is more a preference for a certain kind of style than an accurate critique of the merits of Beattie's prose techniques; at issue, too, is the failure of many critics to realize, as Lionel Trilling points out, that the contrast between "sincerity" as the predominant narrative mode of modernist fiction is at odds with "authenticity" as the leading narrative mode of contemporary fiction.[9] "Affectless" or "deadpan" prose, as some critics choose to describe Beattie's writing style, is characteristic of fiction of the contemporary era, and a failure to recognize this shift in narrative paradigms has often accounted for, not only inaccurate assessments of Beattie's style, but misinterpretations and undervaluings of the character of contemporary narrative technique in general.

In an illuminating discussion of contemporary fiction, Bill Oliver states that "two of the most frequent narrative styles in contemporary fiction" are "the univocal and the equivocal." The univocal "bespeaks an imagination which subsumes details under a controlling idea. Through its confidential tone and self-referring vocabulary and figures of speech, it promotes a particular view of reality and encourages the reader to share that view." The equivocal voice, by contrast, "denotes an imagination which revels in details and resists controlling ideas. Through its pervasive irony and eclectic language, it suggests the inadequacy of any particular viewpoint. Instead of offering conclusions about reality, it poses various hypotheses and refers the reader to his own experience for verification."[10] In terms of Oliver's schema, the univocal voice would be more characteristic of lyrical writers, such as Fitzgerald or Thomas Wolfe, while the equivocal voice best describes the narrative style of Hemingway. Thus, it is interesting that what critics eagerly praise in Hemingway—the sparse, almost skeletal prose style, the accumulation of descriptive detail (both physical and psychological), the objective, nonintrusive narrative stance—they condemn in neorealist writers like Ann Beattie or Raymond Carver.

Oliver further notes that "clinical detachment is one mark of the equivocal voice, which levels distinctions, treating one detail more or less like another. . . . In this way, the narrator can collect data indefinitely, without having to judge its relative importance. Instead of a unified picture, he produces an accumulation of facts." Moreover, as Oliver points out, "the continual accumulation of facts disorients the reader, but that, too, is part of the equivocal narrator's intent. He discredits particular viewpoints, thus keeping the reader off balance."

In contemporary fiction, the narrator often discovers "aimlessly exhausting permutations of meaning" because the author "cannot assume that he and his readers agree on man's nature and destiny, and, therefore, he cannot rely upon a shared universe of discourse to ease communication. As Wayne Booth and others have pointed out, "the discourse of the Victorian novel has long since been replaced by mutual distrust and confusion between novelist and reader and a subsequent devaluation of language."[11] The expectation that fiction should present a coherent world view has been replaced in contemporary fiction by the sense that the world is too fragmented to be encompassed by any world view. Philosophical relativism, ambiguity, emotional neutrality, and the belief that "the way man uses (or misuses) language . . . is the most telling symptom of what is wrong with human nature"[12] characterize contemporary fiction in the same way that a focus upon self-contained world views and moralistic answers defined the fiction of earlier periods.

A number of critics, most especially Gilder, have attacked Beattie for the ambivalent tone of her writings and for the deliberately ambiguous nature of the endings in both her stories and her novels.[13] This type of attack is levelled against a particular fictional mode rather than against the actual merit of what Beattie has achieved by working within its parameters. Neat, facile, moralistic endings are the philosophical result of a consistent world view in which all the paradoxes and ambiguities of existence can be reconciled and resolved. In contemporary fiction, the focus is upon showing how and why "the center will not hold," rather than upon offering clearly defined perspectives upon that center. This shift in paradigmatic emphasis is a crucial one, and one that is often overlooked or denied in assessments of Beattie's fiction.

Critics do note, with a measure of accuracy, that the methodology of the equivocal voice is far more effective for and appropriate to the short story than it is to the novel. An emphasis upon shifting narrative perspectives, ambiguity, and narration through the accumulation of detail would seem, logically, to be more powerful in shorter narrative forms in which compression is the key literary technique, than in the novel, in which expansion is the essential mode. Critics rightly assert that Beattie is a far better short story writer than a novelist. Beattie shares that perspective and has commented, "I really do feel like a bumbler with the novel form. . . . I wonder if there *are* novelists who feel they know how to write novels. I wonder if this knowledge exists. At least there must be people who are not petrified of attempting it, who think of the work they're going to do automatically in terms of its being turned into a novel."[14] Elsewhere she added, "I really wish I knew how to write novels. I wish someone had 10 rules we could follow."[15]

In fairness to Beattie, however, it should be noted that her responses and the responses of critics were directed at *Chilly Scenes of Winter* and *Falling in Place,* both structurally amorphous novels that indicate a less precise control of materials and narrative perspective than *Love Always.* *Love Always* is a highly focused novel, indicative of both Beattie's greater control over narrative and thematic materials and detail and her greater sophistication in using the novel form. Unlike *Falling in Place,* which is a sprawling and somewhat disjointed novel, *Love Always* reveals the compression of technique and focus usually found only in Beattie's short stories. The unified structure and the narrative precision of *Love Always* vitiate, if not totally contradict, Beattie's assertion that she is a "bumbler" with the novel form.

When critics search for analogs by means of which to determine Beattie's literary merit and the quality of her achievement, they compare her to Hemingway for style and focus, and to J. D. Salinger, John Cheever, and John Updike for an emphasis upon social realism and an attempt to capture the ethos of a particular era. While these comparisons are certainly accurate in focusing upon certain aspects of Beattie's writings, the writer whose works Beattie's most resemble in fictional design is F. Scott Fitzgerald.

Sheila Weller has noted the emphasis upon a "new lost generation" in Beattie's fiction,[16] just as "the lost generation" was the central concern in Fitzgerald's fictive universe. Aimlessness, drifting, alienation, passivity, the inability to communicate on a deep level or to share emotional intimacy were also major themes in Fitzgerald's writings. In both writers, too, there is a strong, underlying theme of the romantic

quest. Beattie's characters are not happy to be lost in a cultural wasteland; they long for something greater, something more meaningful, to
capture their imaginations and infuse their lives with purpose. They
are Nicks or Gatsbys, either lost in the decadence and acquiescing, or
searching vainly after a Platonic idea of beauty, truth, or love that can
fulfill the longing that defines and spurs their existence. Like Fitzgerald's characters, they see through the emptiness of their era, at the same
time they are products of the era they find so vacuous and spiritually
unfulfilling.

If Fitzgerald was the social historian, the literary chronicler, of the
generation that came to consciousness in the 1920s, Beattie is the same
type of historian and chronicler of the generation whose sense of self
and of purpose in life was defined by the values and beliefs of the
1960s. Pico Iyer describes Beattie's characters as "well-heeled Lonelyhearts, raised on expectations they frequently let down." The description could apply equally as well to Fitzgerald's characters, especially
those in *The Great Gatsby*. Iyer describes Beattie's characters in this
fashion: "Sprung loose from certainties without being swept up by revolution, old enough to have witnessed turmoil, yet too young to have
joined or beaten it, they find themselves stranded in that famous space
between two worlds, one dying, the other powerless to be born."[17] The
description could just as aptly apply to Fitzgerald's "lost generation,"
for emotional and spiritual enervation is a central concern in his fiction
as well.

Critics are fond of condemning Beattie for refusing to provide answers in her fiction to the moral and spiritual crises of the contemporary era; yet, one can legitimately impose the same type of criticism
upon Fitzgerald, for what type of answers to the wasteland of modern
civilization are provided in *The Great Gatsby* or in *Tender is the Night?*
The emphasis in both writers is not upon answers but upon honest and
moving portrayals, and both Fitzgerald and Beattie are effective in
reflecting the reality that surrounds them. Fitzgerald reveals the decadence of his era by showing his characters partying amidst the chaos.
The party that brings characters to Gatsby's house is a comment upon
an era that wanted to be distracted from reality and that preferred to
embrace frivolity and superficiality at the expense of self-definition and
purpose. In *Love Always,* Beattie adopts the same technique. Hildon
and Maureen, the 1980s inheritors of the American dream, throw lav-
ish parties to which people come to act stylishly false and perfunctorily
insincere. Amidst the gaiety, we perceive the tragedy that contempo-

rary society has become a wasteland, a valley of ashes, but this time, even Dr. T. J. Eckleburg is not watching over to certify the decline. Instead, there is only *Country Daze,* dispensing its pseudowisdom and pseudocompassion with the same penchant for style over substance, flair over purpose, that characterizes both its staff and the era they represent.

If one comment captures the essence of the period and the reason for its decline, it is uttered by the doctor who breaks the news of Jane's death to Priggy Proctor. The doctor states that the name of *Passionate Intensity,* the soap opera Nicole stars in as Stephanie Sykes, must come from the line in Yeats's "Second Coming": "The best lack all conviction, while the worst are full of passionate intensity" (167). The line captures the character of both Fitzgerald's "lost generation" and Beattie's "new lost generation." In Beattie's case the line is even more poignant in view of the fact that the "passionate intensity" of the contemporary age has been reduced to a soap opera that distorts passion into a marketable commodity and twists human values for the sake of TV ratings and sponsors' endorsements. Fitzgerald's industrial valley of ashes is now Beattie's electronic valley of "soapsuds," and the decadence of the contemporary era is captured in a soap-opera version of what conviction and passionate intensity have become.

Blanche H. Gelfant has commented that the achievement of Beattie's writings is "the way they fill the silence that remains when the song is over, the way they say *nothing* when there is nothing to say."[18] Thomas Griffith would have us "rejoice" both for Beattie's statements and her silences, noting that:

Maybe she and the counterculture she describes have the right of it: we are beyond expecting answers to complaints about modern life that, though sweeping, are not clearly formulated. No doubt we influence events less than we used to think we could; even an effort to make any real sense out of our situation may be beyond our means. I'm less certain than I used to be that the "real world" journalists describe—the world of prime ministers, economists, missiles, and charts—has the coherence we try to find in it. As for hoping to influence it much, our opportunities are only hypotheses that can sometimes be made to work. I'm not here to lecture Ann Beattie's characters if she won't. And then it occurs to me that Ann Beattie herself isn't just sitting there, stoned in indecision and rejection like her characters, but that she thinks it valuable to describe that world, and important to get it right. Rejoice, I think, rejoice.[19]

With Griffith, one can "rejoice" that Beattie's sense of the contemporary era, as expressed both through words and silence, is as keen as it is, and that she has captured the ethos of her age in the same fashion that Fitzgerald and Hemingway detailed the 1920s and Salinger, Cheever, and Updike portrayed the malaise of post–World War II America. As a neorealist, and a powerful and talented writer, Beattie has affirmed, once more, fiction's capacity to mirror reality and to reveal both the decadence and the pathos of a given era. And, by the strength of her neorealistic portrayals of contemporary society, Beattie has vouchsafed fiction's capacity to serve as a temporary stay against confusion and defeat. "Rejoice," Griffith has stated, for, amidst "the burning house" that is contemporary society, Beattie is urging, "Aim for grace."

Notes and References

Preface

1. Pico Iyer, "The World According to Beattie," *Partisan Review* 50, no. 4 (1983): 550.

Chapter One

1. Joyce Maynard, "Visiting Ann Beattie," *New York Times Book Review,* 11 May 1980, 39.
2. David M. Taylor, "Ann Beattie," *Dictionary of Literary Biography Yearbook 1982* (Detroit: Gale Research Co., 1983), 207.
3. Michiko Kakutani, "Portrait of the Artist as a First Novelist," *New York Times Book Review,* 8 June 1980, 39.
4. G. E. Murray, "A Conversation with Ann Beattie," *Story Quarterly* 7/8 (1978): 63.
5. Kakutani, "Portrait," 39.
6. J. D. O'Hara, *"Chilly Scenes of Winter, Distortions,"* New York Times Book Review, 15 August 1976, 14.
7. Jay Parini, "A Writer Comes of Age," *Horizon* (December 1982) 22–24.
8. Murray, "Conversation," 63.
9. Parini, "Writer Comes of Age," 22.
10. "The Hum inside the Skull—A Symposium," *New York Times Book Review,* 13 May 1984, 1.
11. Parini, "Writer Comes of Age," 22.
12. Murray, "Conversation," 63.
13. Parini, "Writer Comes of Age," 22.
14. Murray, "Conversation," 64.
15. Mary Vespa, "Once a Cub among the Literary Bears, Ann Beattie Finds Her Career Falling in Place," *People,* 16 June 1980, 68.
16. Murray, "Conversation," 66.
17. Parini, "Writer Comes of Age," 22.
18. John Skow, review of *Head over Heels, Time,* 5 November 1979, 98.
19. Renata Adler, review of *Head over Heels, New Yorker,* 26 November 1979, 172.
20. Taylor, "Ann Beattie," 210.
21. Ibid.
22. Murray, "Conversation," 64.
23. Vespa, "Once a Cub," 68.

ANN BEATTIE

24. Ibid., 67.
25. Murray, "Conversation," 64.
26. Larry McCaffery and Sinda Gregory, "A Conversation with Ann Beattie," *Literary Review* 27 (Winter 1984): 169.
27. "The Hum inside the Skull," 1.
28. McCaffery and Gregory, "Conversation," 176.
29. Ibid, 169–70.
30. Murray, "Conversation," 65.
31. Ibid., 68.

Chapter Two

1. Mas'ud Zavarzadeh, *The Mythopoeic Reality* (Urbana: University of Illinois Press, 1976), vii.
2. Ibid., 33.
3. Ibid., 3.
4. Ibid., 3–4; the quotation is from Alain Robbe-Grillet, *For a New Novel,* trans. Richard Howard (New York: Grove Press, 1965), 19.
5. Zbigniew Brzezinski, *Between Two Ages* (New York: Viking Press, 1971), 9.
6. Zavarzadeh, *The Mythopoeic Reality,* 7.
7. Annie Dillard, *Living by Fiction* (New York: Harper & Row, 1982), 23.
8. For a fuller discussion, see Jonathan Culler, *Structuralist Poetics* (London: Routledge, 1975) and James R. Pinnells, "Theme and the Novel: A Homological Approach," *Dalhousie Review* 62 (Winter 1982–83): 583–99.
9. Roland Barthes, "Authors and Writers," in *Critical Essays,* trans. Richard Howard (Evanston: Northwestern University Press, 1972), 145.
10. Joe David Bellamy, *Superfiction, or the American Story Transformed* (New York: Random House, 1975), 4.
11. Ibid., 3.
12. Jerome Klinkowitz, *The Life of Fiction* (Urbana: University of Illinois Press, 1977), 23.
13. For a fuller discussion, see Philip Stevick, *Alternative Pleasures: Postrealist Fiction and the Tradition* (Urbana: University of Illinois Press, 1981).
14. Joshua Gilder, "Less is Less," *New Criterion* 2 (February 1983): 78.
15. Ibid., 80.
16. Ibid., 82.
17. John Gardner, *On Moral Fiction* (New York: Basic Books, 1978), 18–19.
18. Ibid., 5–6.
19. Joan Didion, *Telling Stories* (Berkeley: The Friends of the Bancroft Library, University of California, 1978), 9.
20. McCaffery and Gregory, "Conversation," 168.

21. Parini, "Writer Comes of Age, 24.
22. Taylor, "Ann Beattie" 208.
23. Ibid., 207.
24. Maynard, "Visiting Ann Beattie" 39.
25. Parini, "Writer Comes of Age," 24.
26. Taylor, "Ann Beattie," 206.
27. Murray, "Conversation," 65.
28. Joshua Gilder, "Down and Out: The Stories of Ann Beattie," *New Criterion* 1 (October 1982): 51.
29. Ibid., 51–52.
30. Ibid., 52.
31. Ibid., 51–54.

Chapter Three

1. Brian Wicker, *The Story-Shaped World: Fiction and Metaphysics* (Notre Dame, Ind.: University of Notre Dame Press, 1975).
2. Maynard, "Visiting Ann Beattie," 39–40.
3. Ibid.
4. *Distortions* (New York: Doubleday, 1976), 14. Subsequent page references will appear within parentheses in the text.
5. McCaffery and Gregory, "Conversation," 174.
6. Maynard, "Visiting Ann Beattie," 41.
7. Parini, "Writer Comes of Age," 24.
8. Ibid., 23.
9. John Romano, "Ann Beattie and the 60's" *Commentary*, February 1977, 63.
10. Ibid.
11. Ibid.
12. Ibid.
13. Gilder, "Down and Out," 51.
14. Ibid., 54–56.
15. Ibid., 56.
16. Peter Glassman, review of *Distortions*, *Hudson Review* 30, no. 3 (1977): 447.
17. Ibid.
18. Larry Husten, "On Ann Beattie," *Salmagundi* 40 (1978): 164.
19. Ibid., 161.
20. Ibid.

Chapter Four

1. Murray, "Conversation," 63.
2. John Updike, review of *Chilly Scenes of Winter*, *New Yorker*, 29 November 1976, 164–66.

3. Benjamin DeMott, *Surviving the 70's* (New York: E. P. Dutton, 1971), 67.

4. *Chilly Scenes of Winter* (New York: Doubleday, 1976), 14. Subsequent page references will appear in parentheses in the text.

5. Maynard, "Visiting Ann Beattie," 40.

6. Taylor, "Ann Beattie," 209.

7. Murray, "Conversation," 66.

8. Updike, review, 164.

9. O'Hara, *"Chilly Scenes,"* 14, 18.

10. David Thorburn, "Recent Novels: Realism Redux," *Yale Review* 76 (Summer 1977): 585–86.

11. Sheila Weller, "A Valentine to the Guys who Grew Up in the '60s," *Ms.*, December 1976, 47.

12. Romano, "Ann Beattie," 64.

Chapter Five

1. Laurie Stone, "Distended Families," review of *Secrets and Surprises, Village Voice,* 26 March 1979, 86.

2. *Secrets and Surprises* (New York: Random House, 1978), 213–14. Subsequent page references will appear in parentheses in the text.

3. Stone, "Distended Families," 86.

4. Ibid., 86.

5. John Gerlach, "Through 'The Octascope': A View of Ann Beattie," *Studies in Short Fiction* 17 (Fall 1980): 490.

6. Ibid., 489–92.

7. Ibid., 492.

8. Stone, "Distended Families," 87.

9. Lee K. Abbott, *The Heart Never Fits Its Wanting* (Cedar Falls, Iowa: North American Review Press, 1980).

10. Weller, "Valentine," 45–47.

11. Karla M. Hammond, "Ann Beattie: Still with the Sixties," *Denver Quarterly* 15, no. 2 (1980): 116.

12. Ibid., 115–16.

13. Stone, "Distended Families," 87.

14. Dean Flower, "Picking up the Pieces," *Hudson Review* 32, no. 2 (1979): 293.

15. Ibid., 295.

Chapter Six

1. Phoebe-Lou Adams, "Life and Letters: Falling in Place," *Atlantic Monthly,* June 1980, 93.

2. Review of *Falling in Place, Wilson Library Bulletin* 54 (June 1980): 675.

3. Richard Locke, "Keeping Cool," *New York Times Book Review*, 11 May 1980, 38.

4. Kate Flint, "The Pickled Worm," *Times Literary Supplement*, 27 March 1981, 333.

5. Campbell Geeslin, review of *Tracer* by Frederick Barthelme, *People*, 26 August 1985, 21–22.

6. Neil Schmitz, "Three Novels," *Partisan Review* 48, no. 4 (1981): 632.

7. Locke, "Keeping Cool," 1.

8. Gilder, "Down and Out," 56.

9. Iyer, "World According to Beattie," 551.

10. *Falling in Place* (New York: Random House, 1980), 13–14. Subsequent page references will appear in parentheses in the text.

11. Georgia A. Brown, "Chilly Views of Beattie," *Canto* 3 (January 1981): 170–71.

12. Robert Towers, "Period Fiction," *New York Times Book Review*, 15 May 1980, 32.

13. Ibid.

14. John Calvin Batchelor, "Queen of the Passive," *Village Voice*, 2 June 1980, 38.

15. Ibid.

16. Batchelor, 38; Towers, 32.

17. Jack Beatty, review of *Falling in Place*, *New Republic*, 7 June 1980, 35.

18. Brown, "Chilly Views," 165–66.

19. Batchelor, "Queen, " 38.

20. Ibid.

21. Brown, "Chilly Views," 166, 169.

22. Ibid., 172–73.

23. Locke, "Keeping Cool," 38.

24. Janet Wiehe, review of *Falling in Place*, *Library Journal*, 15 April 1980, 998.

25. Ibid., 998–99.

26. McCaffery and Gregory, "Conversation," 166.

27. Ibid., 167.

Chapter Seven

1. Iyer, "World According to Beattie," 550.

2. Daniel Zitin, review of *The Burning House*, *Nation*, 30 October 1982, 442.

3. Dean Flower, review of *The Burning House*, *Hudson Review* 36, no. 2 (1983): 359.

4. Iyer, "World According to Beattie," 550.

5. Flower, review, 361.

6. *The Burning House* (New York: Random House, 1982), 243. Subsequent page references will appear in parentheses in the text.

7. McCaffery and Gregory, "Conversation," 166–67.

8. Sanford Pinsker, review of *The Burning House, Studies in Short Fiction* 20 (Spring/Summer 1983): 144.

9. Flower, review, 360.

10. Ibid., 359.

11. Zitin, review, 441.

12. Pearl K. Bell, review of *Falling in Place, Commentary,* July 1980, 59.

13. Zitin, review, 441.

Chapter Eight

1. Josh Rubin, "Having It All," *New York Review of Books,* 18 July 1985, 40–41.

2. *Love Always* (New York: Random House, 1985), 10. Subsequent page references will appear in parentheses in the text.

3. Alice Hoffman, review of *Love Always, New York Times Book Review,* 2 June 1985, 7.

4. Laura Mathews, review of *Love Always, Glamour,* June 1985, 176.

5. Suzanne Hart, review of *Love Always, Vogue,* June 1985, 148.

6. Peter S. Prescott, review of *Love Always, Newsweek,* 17 June 1985, 81.

7. Ibid.

8. Ibid.

9. Hoffman, review, 7.

10. Murray, "Conversation," 66.

11. Gilder, "Down and Out," 56.

12. Mathews, review, 176.

13. Hoffman, review, 7; 44.

Chapter Nine

1. McCaffery and Gregory, "Conversation," 172.

2. Mathews, review, 176.

3. McCaffery and Gregory, "Conversation," 174.

4. Joseph Epstein, "Ann Beattie and the Hippoisie," *Commentary,* March 1983, 55.

5. Whitney Balliett, review of *Falling in Place, New Yorker,* 9 June 1980, 149.

6. David Kubal, review of *Falling in Place, Hudson Review* 30, no. 3 (1980): 444.

7. Beatty, review, 34.

8. Gilder, "Down and Out," 54.

9. Lionel Trilling, *Sincerity and Authenticity* (London: Oxford University Press, 1972).

10. Bill Oliver, "A Manner of Speaking: Percy's Lancelot," *Southern Literary Journal* 15 (Spring 1983): 8.

11. Ibid., 14–16.

12. Ibid., 8.

13. Gilder, "Down and Out," 51–56; see also Kubal; Beatty; and Epstein, 55.

14. Maynard, "Visiting Ann Beattie," 41.

15. Murray, "Conversation," 67.

16. Weller, "Valentine," 47.

17. Iyer, "World According to Beattie," 548–49.

18. Blanche H. Gelfant, "Ann Beattie's Magic Slate, or the End of the Sixties," *New England Review* 1 (1979): 375.

19. Thomas Griffith, "Rejoice If You Can," *Atlantic Monthly,* September 1980, 29.

Selected Bibliography

PRIMARY SOURCES

1. Novels

Chilly Scenes of Winter. New York: Doubleday, 1976. Reprint. New York: Fawcett Popular Library, 1978, (paperback); New York: Warner Books, 1983 (paperback).

Falling in Place. New York: Random House, 1980. Reprint. New York: Fawcett Popular Library, 1980 (paperback); London: Secker & Warburg, 1981; Harmondsworth: Penguin, 1982 (paperback); New York: Warner Books, 1983 (paperback).

Love Always. New York: Random House, 1985. Reprint. London: Joseph, 1985.

2. Short Stories

Distortions. New York: Doubleday, 1976. Reprint. New York: Fawcett Popular Library, 1979 (paperback); New York: Warner Books, 1976 and 1983 (paperback).

Jacklighting. Metacom Limited Editions Series, no. 3. Worcester, Mass.: Metacom Press, 1981.

Secrets and Surprises. New York: Random House, 1978. Reprint. New York: Fawcett Popular Library, 1978 (paperback); London: Hamilton, 1979; New York: Warner Books, 1983 (paperback).

The Burning House. New York: Random House, 1982. Reprint. New York: Ballantine, 1982 (paperback); London: Secker & Warburg, 1983.

SECONDARY SOURCES

1. Interviews

Maynard, Joyce. "Visiting Ann Beattie." *New York Times Book Review,* 11 May 1980, 39–41. A discussion of Beattie's views of her literary career and critical reputation; especially interesting for Beattie's perspectives upon the writing of *Falling in Place.*

McCaffery, Larry and **Sinda Gregory.** "A Conversation with Ann Beattie." *Literary Review* 27 (Winter 1984): 165–77. Significant for Beattie's discussion of her "mannered" prose style and the overall focus of her work upon the breakdown of communications in human relationships.

Miner, Bob. "Ann Beattie: 'I Write Best When I Am Sick.'" *Village Voice,* 9 August 1976, 33–34. Focuses, in large measure, upon Beattie's reputation as a counterculture writer and upon the techniques Beattie employs in structuring her fiction.

Murray, G. E. "A Conversation with Ann Beattie." *Story Quarterly* 7/8 (1978): 62–68. Emphasizes *Distortions* and *Chilly Scenes of Winter;* Murray espouses the view that "faith and despair" are the major themes in Beattie's fiction. Beattie talks about the concepts of illusions and disillusionment in Charles's quest for Laura in *Chilly Scenes of Winter.*

2. Articles

Bell, Pearl K. "Literary Waifs." *Commentary,* February 1979, 67–71. Considers Beattie's "literary waifs" to be in the tradition of John Cheever; "Miss Beattie tells us what happened to the children of Shady Hill and Proxmire Manor."

———. "Marge Piercy and Ann Beattie." *Commentary,* July 1980, 59–61. Contrasts Beattie's *Falling in Place* with Marge Piercy's *Vida;* finds Piercy's world "is a place of heady conflicts between absolutes," while Beattie, "at the opposite extreme, sees a world devoid of all such schematic fitness and order, political or otherwise."

Brown, Georgia A. "Chilly Views of Beattie." *Canto* 3 (January 1981): 165–73. Praises Beattie's distinctive prose style for capturing the essence of lives enmeshed in vacillation and ennui, but finds that Beattie's emphasis upon lives of "quiet desperation" only deals in "surfaces and images—in fashion, and in the fashionable emotions of nostalgia and sentimentality."

Epstein, Joseph. "Ann Beattie and the Hippoisie." *Commentary,* March 1983, 54–58. Envisions Beattie's primary subject as "the fate of her own generation, the generation that was in college and graduate school in the late 60's and early 70's." Beattie's emphasis upon disillusionment and defeat arises from the fact that hers was "a generation of promise," yet one unable to find purpose, direction and self-definition in the 1970s and 1980s.

Gelfant, Blanche H. "Ann Beattie's Magic Slate, or The End of the Sixties." *New England Review* 1 (1979): 374–84. Analyzes *Chilly Scenes of Winter* and selected stories from *Distortions;* finds that Beattie, like J. D. Salinger, "values childlike innocence, precociousness, and whimsy," and is at her best when "she tells stories that embody these qualities while she shows them imperilled."

Gerlach, John. "Through 'The Octascope': A View of Ann Beattie." *Studies in Short Fiction* 17 (Fall 1980): 489–94. An extended critical analysis of Beattie's short story "The Octascope" in *Secrets and Surprises;* finds the male characters in "The Octascope" and in Beattie's fiction in general to be suffering from a kind of passivity that makes them unable to form strong commitments; Beattie's fiction demonstrates "the need for personal growth while depicting the allure of retreat and security."

Gilder, Joshua. "Down and Out: The Stories of Ann Beattie." *New Criterion* 1 (October 1982): 51–56. Severely criticizes Beattie's fiction for failing to offer viable moral solutions to the philosophical problems raised in her fiction; finds Beattie's prose lifeless and tedious and her themes vapid and ephemeral.

————. "Less is Less." *New Criterion* 2 (February 1983): 78–82. A general discussion of minimalism and of such minimalist authors as Beattie, Raymond Carver, and Mary Robison. Minimalism, with its emphasis upon a "constriction" of artistic vision, represents "a kind of literary personal bankruptcy."

Griffith, Thomas. "Rejoice If You Can." *Atlantic Monthly,* September 1980, 28–29. Counters the prevailing view of Beattie as a pessimistic and defeatist writer by arguing that her portrayals of the problems of her generation offer insight into the contemporary psyche and therefore hope for personal growth and change.

Hammond, Karla M. "Ann Beattie: Still with the Sixties." *Denver Quarterly* 15, no. 2 (1980): 115–17. Beattie's fiction chronicles the "sense of desperation entailed in choice" and emphasizes "nihilistic environments" and "a feeling of entrapment."

Iyer, Pico. "The World According to Beattie." *Partisan Review* 50, no. 4 (1983): 548–53. Like J. D. Salinger, John Cheever, and John Updike, Beattie coolly chronicles "the sad eccentricities, plaintive longings, and quiet frustrations" of a generation.

Parini, Jay. "A Writer Comes of Age." *Horizon* December 1982, 22–24. Surveys Beattie's accomplishments in fiction from *Distortions* through *The Burning House* and praises Beattie for her sociological realism and psychological insight; provides useful biographical information on Beattie.

Romano, John. "Ann Beattie & the 60's." *Commentary,* February 1977, 62–64. Beattie's subject matter is "a certain shiftlessness and lack of self-apprehension besetting people in their twenties and thirties"; Beattie "conveys the drabness of these lives by her tone and an almost hallucinatory particularity of detail."

Taylor, David M. "Ann Beattie." *Dictionary of Literary Biography Yearbook 1982.* Detroit: Gale Research Co., 1983, 206–12. A biographical and critical discussion; Beattie's fiction focuses upon capturing the essence of lives composed of "indirection, indecision, and angst."

Index